# LEGAL SEX

*Other Books by L. E. Rozovsky*

**Canadian Hospital Law: A Practical Guide**
**Canadian Manual on Hospital By-Laws** (with W. M. Dunlop)
**Canadian Hospital Law,** 2nd edition
**The Canadian Patient's Book of Rights**

# LEGAL SEX

L. E. and F. A. Rozovsky

DOUBLEDAY CANADA LIMITED
Toronto, Canada

DOUBLEDAY & COMPANY, INC.
Garden City, New York

1982

Library of Congress Catalog Card Number: 80-2981

Copyright © 1982 by L. E. and F. A. Rozovsky

All Rights Reserved

First Edition

**Canadian Cataloguing in Publication Data**

Rozovsky, Lorne Elkin, 1942-
  Legal sex

Includes index.
ISBN 0-385-17415-2 (Hardcover)
ISBN 0-385-17416-0 (Paperback)

1. Sex and law—Canada—Popular works.
I. Rozovsky, F. A. (Fay Adrienne), 1950-
II. Title.

KE8928.Z82R69        345.71′0253        C81-095136-3


Printed in Canada by Alger Press Limited
Typeset by ART-U Graphics
Designed by Irene Carefoot

*To our parents, who made it all possible*

**WARNING!**

THIS BOOK IS INTENDED TO MAKE THE READER
AWARE OF VARIOUS ASPECTS OF CANADIAN LAW AS
IT AFFECTS SEX AS OF SEPTEMBER 1, 1981.
IT IS NOT TO REPLACE ADVICE GIVEN BY A LAWYER
WHICH IS SPECIFICALLY DESIGNED FOR A PAR-
TICULAR SET OF CIRCUMSTANCES TAKING INTO
CONSIDERATION THE SPECIFICS OF LOCAL LEGIS-
LATION, AND LOCAL LAW GENERALLY.

# Preface

If it were not for sex, where would civilization be? We do not mean the act of sexual intercourse, either for pleasure or for procreation. The answer in either of these cases is fairly obvious. We are referring to the *subject* of sex.

Sex is the hottest box office topic in the world. Without it, we would not have a wealth of world literature, painting, the dance, cinema, sculpture, television—the list is endless. A great deal of human expression has sexual overtones, whether it be found on the stage of the Stratford Festival, or on the cubicle dividers of a tavern washroom in Vancouver or St. John's.

Sex has been analyzed to death by psychologists, psychiatrists, sociologists, anthropologists and the dozens of other "-ologists" who cram the universities and deplete the funds of the Humanities Research Council. Despite this, as we travel across Canada giving legal seminars, press interviews and consultations, we are constantly asked for a lawyer's view of sex. We are asked for this view in language that is stripped of the mumbo jumbo of the "-ologists" and the "legalese" of the lawyer. The questioners want the answers in ordinary, plain English that can be understood by the average, reasonably intelligent Canadian. That is why we wrote this book.

Our thanks must go first to the thousands of people from Victoria, British Columbia to St. Anthony, Newfoundland who have attended our seminars and conferences, and who have encouraged us to write this book. Particular thanks go to Mr. George McCurdy, the executive director of the Nova Scotia Human Rights Commission and Leslie Samson and Philip Comeau of the Commission who assembled an enormous amount of material for us and encouraged us. We also thank Ann Frank of Fort Lauderdale, Dr. David B. Shires of Halifax,

Virginia Beaton of Portuguese Cove, Nova Scotia and Professor Clare Beckton for their advice and some very sparkling suggestions, as well as Nadine Cooper Mont of the Nova Scotia Department of Consumer Affairs.

We are also indebted to Debbie Innes for her patience and care in preparing the manuscript and to Hy Rozovsky for his proofreading and encouragement.

If, despite all of the help and encouragement we have received, there are still errors, omissions or parts that are unclear, the fault lies with the authors.

**Lorne Elkin Rozovsky**
**Fay Adrienne Rozovsky**
**Halifax, Nova Scotia**

# Contents

# LEGAL SEX

# 1 What is Law? What is Sex? A Serious Legal Question

"There oughta be a law!" people scream. The cry against immorality and indecency was heard 100 years ago, and despite the coming of the "do-your-own-thing" generation, the cry is still heard. The flower children of the 1960s have had their impact but the Imperial Order of Daughters of the Empire and the Catholic Women's League are still representative of millions of Canadians.

It is true that what society and law would not tolerate even 20 years ago is permitted and even flaunted today. The exotic dancers at Toronto's Casino Theatre in the 1950s were never naked. Today, both men and women dance naked in at least some Canadian bars. The condom was the unspoken device of the sophisticated couple and the soldier on leave. It is now advertised in college newspapers to teenagers in love, along with pregnancy counseling for those who forgot.

Despite this openness, or what some would call liberality, there are millions who say, "There oughta be a law!" and there is. Ontario, by law, insists on cuts in major motion pictures that are shown untouched in Quebec and Nova Scotia. With full legal authority, school boards remove best-selling Canadian novels from library shelves.

The questions that challenge us are: When, as our prime minister has said, does the law have "no business in the bedrooms of the nation?" When has the law no business at all, anywhere, anytime, involving anybody? Why do at least some of us say that "there oughta be a law" and at other times not?

There are three major reasons for passing laws in the area of sex. The first is to combat immorality. Laws forbidding sexual relations between people of the same sex, sodomy, and indecent performances fall into this category. The second is to protect the innocent or those who cannot protect themselves. For this reason, laws over the years have been passed to prohibit sexual relations with youngsters, or with women who are dependent on men, such as lady passengers with the captain of their ship. The third reason is to protect society. This reason may spring from the other two. It is felt that a proliferation of immoral conduct will weaken family life and the fabric of society and, like Rome, lead to its downfall. Failure to protect the defenseless, it is argued, will lead to anarchy and social disintegration.

The problem with immorality is that not everyone agrees on what is immoral. People argue that standards of morality are eternal. Philosophically this may be true, but what was tolerated years ago may not be today, as is witnessed by current attitudes towards slavery, or the castration of young boys to preserve their soprano voices for the opera. What was considered scandalous even a few years ago is acceptable today. A middle-aged woman in Quebec in the 1940s and 1950s could be arrested for wearing Bermuda shorts in her own backyard, but not today.

Even today, there are few agreed standards of morality. The majority of Canadians probably feel that the idea of two grown men in bed making love to one another is immoral, or disgusting, or at the very least, unappealing. Others would not care one way or the other and still others would actually like it. If law is passed on the basis of public opinion, what is the consensus?

Some may not approve of particular activities, but would not brand them as immoral. A more appropriate label would be, simply, in bad taste. Should the law be the guardian of public taste as it is in the Soviet Union? Attempts have been made even recently in Canada to use law, or at least legal authorization, in this way. Montreal's leading funding agency attempted to close down a production of one of Canada's most distinguished theaters, the Théâtre du Nouveau Monde. The play had religious overtones that some thought were sacrilegious. Is it law based on morality or on taste?

A further problem facing those who advocate legislation on the basis of maintaining at least some level of moral conduct, is that of enforcement. Incest is a crime in this country, but how often is anyone charged, let alone convicted of it? Are we naive enough to think that the lack of enforcement proves that it does not take place? If, however, the difficulty of enforcing a particular law is used as a reason for abolishing the law, such as was advanced for the abolition of prohibition, or currently, for marijuana laws, then perhaps Parliament should abolish laws against theft, criminal negligence and rape. A shockingly small percentage of these offenses result in arrests or convictions. In this day and age crime, more often than not, does pay.

The second rationale for legislation in the sexual area, that is, to protect the innocent and those who cannot protect themselves, also carries difficulties. As with law designed to control morality, there is a problem of enforcement. Someone who cannot defend himself is often in a position not to complain and thus bring the law into force. This has been seen in the battered child situation. The law in most provinces bars children from seeing certain films, but they still get in. Far more women are sexually assaulted than those who complain. Young boys who are seduced, or who seduce other boys or adult men, do not complain. Most young girls who are prohibited by Parliament from having intercourse but who do so anyway, do not lodge a complaint. Is the threat of prosecution controlling the actions of those who might harm the innocent, but who do not? There will never be an answer.

The second problem that accompanies this rationale is that of who is to be protected. Who are the innocent? Who are those who cannot protect themselves? Is the female passenger on a ship in such a defenseless position that she needs legal protection from seduction by the owner, master or employer on board the ship? There are, no doubt, many who need such protection. If a woman is threatened, such an argument can be made, but is the position in itself threatening, so that protection from seduction is required? Some women may be able to fend for themselves. Young men are not protected.

Do female employees need protection from male employers, when male employees do not have it from female employers, or any employees from the homosexual or lesbian advances of their superiors?

Are children really as innocent or as impressionable as we would like to think? Some, no doubt, are. Others can be judged by the graffitti found in school washrooms.

How many people need legal protection (or think they need it) before a law is passed for everyone in that group—those who need it and those who do not?

## Law and Morality

In the 1950s the British Parliament established a Committee on Homosexual Offenses and Prostitution, known as the Wolfenden Committee. The Committee reported on these two matters and how they should be dealt with by the criminal law. In its report, the Committee found the function of criminal law to be "to preserve public order and decency, to protect the citizen from what is offensive or injurious, and to provide sufficient safeguards against exploitation and corruption of others, particularly those who are specially vulnerable because they are young, weak in body or mind, inexperienced, or in a state of special physical, official or economic dependence."

The Committee felt that the criminal law should not be used to prevent what some, or even a majority of people, saw as immoral conduct unless it infringed on someone else. Law and morality are not necessarily the same. Law and ethics are not the same. Despite this essential difference, the public still thinks that morality can be enforced by law.

The Law Reform Commission of Canada recommended that incest be removed from the Criminal Code as a crime unless it occurs by force or with a youngster. The government had to admit that the public outcry was so great against the proposal, that they could not act on it.

To most people incest is a disgusting and immoral act. Therefore, "there oughta be a law." There has been a law for a very long time, but the practice continues. Some say that it is widespread. There are few charges laid however, and few convictions. There are few complaints. Given this situation, why have a law against incest?

Law can never aid society in becoming more civilized. It can only be viewed as a stopgap measure, an attempt to prevent society from slipping below an unacceptable minimum. The public and the politicians often forget this. It is a reflection of society, or at least of that part of society which is involved in affecting social policy and law. That part of society which is not involved is, in effect, giving tacit approval. Prior to the Nazis establishing a police state in Germany, they were able to gain control with the outright support of a minority and the lack of opposition by millions of others.

## What is Law?

Most people think of law as that which is passed by Parliament, a provincial legislature or a municipal council. Also included would be regulations passed by the federal and provincial cabinets, ministers, boards and commissions. These are the laws which are usually of the "thou shalt not" variety, and sometimes of the "thou shalt" type. Failure to abide by this type of law may result in a charge being laid by a Crown prosecutor. If he can convince a judge or a judge and jury beyond a reasonable doubt that the accused has disobeyed the law, a fine or imprisonment may result. This type of law, that is legislation, can also give rights to citizens and corporations, or can take them away.

The "thou shalt not" laws are easier to enforce than the "thou shalt" laws since the wrongful act is conspicuous. Unless the person who sees it occurring complains or it is seen by a government agent, such as a police officer, customs agent or inspector whose job it is to complain, the wrongful act goes unprosecuted and the law might as well not have been passed.

The "thou shalt" laws, such as the requirement that all doctors report all cases of V.D., are even more difficult to enforce. How can the law enforcement agencies know that an act should have taken place when they do not know of the circumstances giving rise to the requirement?

Law, however, is far more than commandments and prohibitions. In all provinces and territories, with the exception of Quebec, most law has never been discussed on the floor of the legislature. It has been developed by judges in this country following the legal traditions passed down from England. These legal principles are derived from court decisions of prior disputes. In determining what the law is or might be in any current legal dispute, lawyers look to prior decisions involving similar situations. There may never have been a situation before the courts which is exactly the same as the current one, so similar situations are used to guide the courts as to the approach that should be applied.

This law, which is constantly developing and adapting itself to new situations, is called the English Common Law. It does not come in the "thou shalt" and "thou shalt not" form. It outlines the rights of people and the duties of others. It states that a patient has a right to refuse a hysterectomy even if she needs one. The doctor has the duty not to operate on her. If he does, she can sue for assault and ask the court to pay her compensation. If she agrees to the operation, she has the right to have it performed, according to a reasonable standard. The surgeon has the duty to perform it reasonably. If he does not and injures her as

a result, she can sue for negligence, and seek compensation from the
doctor for her injuries. (See *The Canadian Patient's Book of Rights* by
L. E. Rozovsky).

In some situations these principles have been altered by legislatures.
The principle of being able to refuse treatment does not apply to
communicable diseases like tuberculosis or syphilis. Every province
has legislation which allows those patients to be forcibly treated.

Many of these principles also apply in Quebec, but not because of
the English Common Law. They are embodied in the Civil Code of
that province which is interpreted and applied to disputes before
Quebec courts.

The main purpose of the law, therefore, is to govern the relations
between people. It also reflects those relations. The relations are made
up of rights and duties. They deal with property, contracts, professional conduct, wills, bodily contact and, of course, sex.

## What about Sex?

The word conjures up interest, curiosity, embarrassment, shock and
laughter depending on who uses it and under what circumstances.
Neither federal nor provincial statutes or regulations define it. In such
cases, when a word is not defined in law, the courts will turn to the way
a word is usually used, which means consulting the dictionary.

Sex is defined by the *Shorter Oxford English Dictionary* as the
distinction between males and females and the sum of those differences
in the structure and function of the reproductive organs. Therefore, it
is the subject which divides human beings into men and women, the
physical and psychological differences and the process by which men
and women relate to one another because of those differences.

Since law is the study of the relations between people and between
people and society, sex and the law is the study of law as it relates to the
sexual differences between human beings and their sexual relations.
Freud believed that all human behavior is sexually based. If this is so,
law, with the exception of subjects such as contracts, tax law and
corporate law, is also.

# 2 Sex How and With Whom?

Under the Criminal Code of Canada, Parliament has made it a criminal offense to perform certain forms of sex. It has also prohibited sex between certain groups of people. Some of the persons with whom sex is banned seem strange and of minimal concern, such as sex with a woman passenger aboard a vessel or sex with dead bodies. Some of the forms of sex which are prohibited appear lewd and perverted to many, such as bestiality and buggery. The list of sexual activities considered criminal, and of the persons who legally cannot engage in sex, is rather short but nonetheless quite broad in its coverage.

To many people, it is shocking that the law is so sweeping in its effect on how sex may be performed and in its prohibition of who may engage in sex. These people think the police, prosecutors and judges have more serious crimes to tackle than sexual matters. They argue that the law really does not reduce (let alone eliminate) sex deemed offensive under the Criminal Code. They wonder why such laws are on the books and how well the criminal provisions are enforced.

It may be of some comfort to those critical of the legal stance on how and with whom sex may be performed to know that the law does have its limits. Sex in private is usually beyond the reach of the Criminal Code. The problem is defining what is an act done in "private?" Does it mean in one's house? In a parked car? In a darkened alley? On a deserted beach?

Given society's rapidly changing attitude towards sex, are the critics correct in attacking the Criminal Code as outdated and unenforceable? Are proponents right in demanding even stricter laws and penalties for sex involving children? Is the Criminal Code the best means available for restricting those sexual acts considered offensive and the people who participate in such behavior?

## Sex How?

In a number of sections in the Criminal Code, Parliament has designated certain types of sex as criminal offenses. The penalties for violating these laws vary from five years' imprisonment for acts of gross indecency to as much as 14 years for buggery and bestiality.

Buggery, as described in the legal dictionaries, is sexual intercourse between a man or a woman with a "brute beast," a man with another man, or a man unnaturally with a woman. Sodomy is also considered an unnatural sex act, but unlike buggery, it has referred to penetration of one man's penis into the anus of another man or boy. Over time, the term has also come to include similar penetration of a woman by a man. Today, buggery and sodomy are often used interchangeably, although in Canada the Criminal Code refers to buggery.

Sodomy is also distinguished from fellatio, the penetration of a man's penis into another person's mouth. Fellatio too is considered a criminal offense punishable as a gross sexual act under the Criminal Code.

Bestiality differs markedly from other sexual acts. It refers specifically to sex between human beings and animals. It is an offense punishable by a long period of imprisonment.

Regardless of the terms used, the Criminal Code punishes unnatural sex acts or what the Common Law referred to as "crimes against nature." Of all the provisions in the Criminal Code referring to "sex how," bestiality and buggery are singled out for the longest jail sentences. This is perhaps a reflection of society's intolerance and abhorrence of such activity.

The Criminal Code also makes it an offense for one male to assault another male with the intent to commit buggery. (For other forms of indecent sexual assaults see Chapter Nine: *Rape and Sexual Assaults*.) It is also a crime for a man to indecently assault another man.

In one case under this section of the Code, four Nova Scotia men were tried and convicted of indecently assaulting a young man. The man, aged 19, was an orphan and boarded with a couple for whom he did housework. Six months earlier he had experienced some "trouble" with two of the defendants. In May 1973 the four stopped and asked the man if he wanted a ride and when he declined, two of them got out and dragged him to the car. The four took him to a secluded location, stripped his clothes from him, and while three of them held him, the fourth attacked his genitals. They then let him get dressed and drove him back to a place near his home. The Crown, believing the punishment given the four too lenient, appealed their sentences. On appeal, Chief Justice MacKeigan of the Nova Scotia Supreme Court said that the sentences should stand. He said that the trial judge, knowing the community, the nature of the offense and the deterrent effect of the publicity surrounding the case, had correctly found imprisonment would do nothing to deter or rehabilitate the defendants. Noting this, and considering that the victim suffered no physical or mental injury, a fine of $500 each and a day in jail was leveled against the four.

Quite a different position was taken by a Manitoba court in a case involving three prisoners charged with gross indecency and indecent assault. The three held a mock trial of another man awaiting psychiatric care while all four were detained at the Winnipeg Public Safety Building. They sentenced him to commit sex acts with them. To enforce the "sentence" they beat the man about his body and threatened to hang him. The Crown appealed what it considered light sentences and the Manitoba Court of Appeal agreed. Mr. Justice Dickson said that the trial judge should not have given lesser sentences because there was insufficient surveillance by guards. Prisoners, the Court of Appeal said, were entitled to as much protection of the law as anyone outside the prison walls. The sentences were lengthened from six months to one and a half years for each of the prisoners.

Why would the Nova Scotia court refuse to increase a sentence for indecent assault on a male when the Manitoba court tripled it? The cases can be reconciled. In the Nova Scotia case, the young man suffered an indignity but no more—there was no physical harm. In the Manitoba situation, the victim was beaten up and threatened with hanging. He was also assaulted sexually by three men. It was a more serious episode. The cases point out that indecent attacks by men against men will trigger criminal charges. The severity of punishment in each case will vary with the facts and harm to the victim.

Acts of gross indecency are an offense under the Criminal Code. Unlike the provision involving assaults by men on other men, this section refers to "every one who commits an act of gross indecency with another person." No assault is mentioned. The activity is not done against another but *with* another person. It is an agreed-to act. The Criminal Code does not define what is an act of "gross indecency" and as with other undefined terms, the courts have provided an interpretation.

One midsummer evening, a police officer happened upon a man and woman in a parked car. The officer claimed that the man's face was wet, covered with what he described as a slime-like or mucous-like substance. The female occupant of the car was equally wet-faced. The couple were charged with gross indecency. At their trial, the Alberta court found the couple not guilty. The evidence presented by the prosecution was that the man's face was laden with mucus from kissing the woman's genitals, while the woman was perspiring from sexual arousal. The judge found that since the police only had 20 seconds in which to view the act, there was insufficient time for the officer to gather enough evidence for a conviction of gross indecency. The court also pointed out that since it had been a warm summer evening and given the fact that they had just been detained by the police, it was not surprising that the couple were perspiring. In remarking on the charge, the judge said that a male implanting a kiss on a woman's external genitalia was not an act of gross indecency under the Criminal Code. What was required for such a conviction was evidence of cunnilingus.

In a Manitoba case, a man was charged with gross indecency when he forcibly committed an act of fellatio with a woman. Evidence in the case indicated that the man virtually peeled the woman's clothes from her body, then in a vice-like manner, fastened his knees about her neck in order to perform the act. While the accused admitted his actions, he tried to defend himself by arguing that this sort of activity was ordinary love-making. He even suggested that animals often perform similar acts. The court was not moved by this defense. The acts of animals, the court said, were not the standard by which to assess human conduct. Since the man's actions were repugnant to ordinary norms of morality and were unnatural and depraved, the judge said it could be described as nothing less than gross indecency.

Sometimes acts which would normally amount to gross indecency fall outside the scope of the Criminal Code. One of the circumstances in which this exception prevails is activity done in private between consenting adults. Questions Canadian courts have had to face are what is meant by "private" and what constitutes a "public place."

The British Columbia Court of Appeal found that an alcove between a set of washrooms at a public beach at 11:40 P.M. *was* a public place. Two men engaging in homosexual activity were found by police in an alcove at an English Bay beach house. The pair were charged with gross indecency. The court said that although the act occurred at night, long after the bath houses had been locked, the area still amounted to a public place. The activity of the two men was clearly visible to the police. Since the act of gross indecency took place within view of others on a well-used beach, open to the public, their homosexual actions could not be said to have been committed in private.

A Quebec court took the opposite position in a case involving two men who were caught in sexual activity together while parked in a car. The vehicle was parked in a parking lot which during daytime hours would be quite visible. The indecent act occurred at 4:30 A.M., however, when few, if any passersby would have seen them. The court acquitted one of the men who had been charged with gross indecency. The act, the court said, was committed with another consenting adult in a car, which is a private place, in an area that was at the time and in the circumstances largely a private place.

If a car is a private place, what about an act of gross indecency visible through the window of a private home? The Manitoba Court of Appeal found a man not guilty of gross indecency when he was arrested for committing fellatio with a woman. The pair, consenting adults, were seen through a window by police who were in the process of carrying out a liquor search warrant. The act was committed at 2:00 A.M. in a private home located in an area devoid of traffic or persons on foot. Had the police not fortuitously happened to catch a glimpse of the pair, they would not have been before the court. Given the facts of the case, the court said the act was done in private and therefore outside the scope of the Criminal Code.

Although the Criminal Code does not define what amounts to gross indecency, the courts seem to know it when they see it. It depends on the circumstances and place (private v. public) of each case. Acts committed in public, which are morally depraved or repugnant, however, usually fit the bill.

## Sex With Dead Bodies

Another section of the Criminal Code prohibits a different sort of indecency from the provision banning gross indecency. This section punishes those who improperly or indecently interfere with a dead body or human remains. It matters not whether the body is buried. Upon conviction, persons causing an indignity to a dead body may be imprisoned for up to five years.

In 1965 this provision under the Criminal Code was used to punish a man who either copulated or attempted to copulate with a dead woman. What the man did not know was that the victim was dead. He believed that she was unconscious. Charged with indignity to a dead body, the man claimed at his trial that while he knew what he was doing physically he was so drunk that he did not know his sexual "favor" was expended upon a dead person. The trial judge did not accept the man's defense and he appealed. The Yukon Territory Court of Appeal affirmed his conviction. It did not matter, the court said, whether or not the man knew his victim was deceased. Since he possessed a criminal intent to rape her if she were alive, he could not then claim he was innocent because the woman was deceased at the time of his indecent behavior.

## Sex with Whom?

The Criminal Code goes into rather great detail about who legally may engage in sex with whom. Some of these provisions are based on what many would consider as rather outdated mores and attitudes existent at a time when women were seen as the weaker sex, totally unequipped to protect themselves. These laws were the product of a genuine, albeit paternalistic, concern for the safety of women rather than the product of a sexist attitude. Today's feminists, however, may cringe at these laws designed to protect them from being unlawfully seduced.

## The Seduction of Women

Even the language of these sections of the Criminal Code harkens back to a time when chastity and virginity were the paramount considerations and preoccupations of those who were in the know. Under one section of the Criminal Code it is still a crime for a man over 18 to seduce a young woman between 16 and 18 years of age who was, prior to the seduction, of chaste character. This offense was (and still is) deemed so offensive that upon conviction a man could receive up to two years' imprisonment!

Similarly, a man of 21 years of age or more can be sent to jail for up to two years, if under a promise to marry he seduces an unmarried woman less than 21 years old. For the charge to stick, the maiden in question must have been of previously chaste character. The promise to marry could not be conditional upon the woman becoming pregnant. "Seduction" means more than illicit sex. It also includes surrender of the young lady's chastity to the accused due to his persistent solicitation, promises, persuasion, bribes or anything short of force.

Another section of the Criminal Code punishes any man who, as the owner, master or employee on board a passenger-carrying vessel seduces a female passenger on the vessel. It also punishes the use of threats or his authority to gain illicit sex with female passengers. This offense, like other seduction crimes, is punishable by up to two years' imprisonment. The Criminal Code, in this respect, represents quite a different standard from that demonstrated by television's "Love Boat!"

## Sex with a Step-Daughter or Female Employee

Some of the Criminal Code prohibitions on sex with certain people may receive the endorsement of even the most ardent feminists despite the motivation for the law. One such law punishes illicit sex by a man with his step-daughter, foster-daughter or female ward. It also prohibits illicit sex between a man and a woman under 21 years of age of previously chaste character in his employ, or subject to his direction or control or from whom such a woman receives her wages either directly or indirectly. When the charge stems from the employment relationship the court may find the man guilty even though the evidence does *not* show that he is more to blame than the woman. This evidence requirement suggests that the honorable Members of Parliament wanted to protect those "vivacious and luscious flowers of chaste youth" who unwittingly or quite consciously brought illicit sex down upon themselves. Paternalistic or not, the law may be a great help in the fight against sexual harrassment on the job in the 1980s.

## Incest

Perhaps one of the most serious concerns facing Canadians today is the growing awareness of incest throughout the country. Countless articles in popular magazines and television documentaries have been presented on the subject. Upon conviction, a person guilty of incest can be put in prison for up to 14 years. The considerable length of the possible maximum prison term indicates how serious an offense incest is considered in relation to other sexual offenses, such as gross indecency or sex with dead bodies.

Only certain categories of relatives can commit incest. The act must take place between a person who knows that another is, by blood relationship, his or her parent, child, brother, sister, half brother, half sister, grandparent or grandchild. Aunts and uncles as well as cousins are not specified in the law. There must be a "blood relationship," which means that adopted children are not protected by the law. Similarly, children conceived with donor sperm or a donated ovum who are involved in illicit sex with their nonbiological parents are excluded from the law.

Certain defenses or exceptions are outlined in the law relating to incest. For example, a male under 14 years of age is deemed incapable of committing such an offense. If a woman is convicted of incest but the court finds that she committed incest because she was under duress, restraint, or fear of her sexual partner, the court need not impose punishment on her.

Incest is generally viewed as a socially and morally repugnant activity. It is hard to control through criminal law since the victim is often afraid or embarrassed to come forward and lodge a complaint. Some argue that the better way to handle incest is through social services, family crisis intervention and intensive counseling. Given the impact incest has upon the victim and the rest of the family, it is questionable whether criminal law, with its so-called "deterrent" effect, is the best means of combating this form of sexual encounter.

## Noncriminal Control of Sex with Whom

Although sex outside of marriage is quite commonplace in today's society, those who follow "tradition" should know that certain restrictions exist governing who may marry whom. Some of these restrictions are based on biblical teachings, while others reflect public health considerations. Most if not all of the provinces prohibit marriage between persons who share a blood relationship. As the statutes in Ontario and Prince Edward Island describe it, persons of specific "degrees of affinity and consanguinity" cannot marry. For example, a man cannot marry his aunt or his son's wife, his sister or nephew's wife. Similarly, a woman cannot marry her uncle or brother, her aunt's husband or her niece's husband.

In some locations, including Saskatchewan and the Northwest Territories, marriage ceremonies cannot be performed if one of the parties has a communicable disease—such as syphilis—that is in an active state. The rationale for the ban is to protect the would-be spouse from unknowingly contracting venereal disease and passing it on to any offspring.

## The Future of Sex How and with Whom

In years to come, it is quite possible that Parliament will repeal or modify greatly the law prohibiting the seduction of female passengers, buggery and bestiality. The rationale has almost been forgotten for these and other Criminal Code sections which ban certain forms of sex and restrict with whom it may be performed. Other laws, however, may become stricter to keep up with changing times. For example, incestuous relationships between adopted children or artificially conceived children and their nonbiological parents may be criminalized. As the ethics and attitudes of society change, attempts will be made to amend the laws regulating sexual relations. Some are bound to take on a different complexion. In reassessing these laws, society and Parliament may well ask if they should attempt to control sex at all, since people will do what they want despite what the laws say.

# 3  Sex Without Children

Everyone seems to want sex. It is the resulting children who are often unwanted. Since time immemorial, religious leaders have been the bedfellows of politicians in exhorting the population to produce, or rather to reproduce. Orthodox Jewish rabbis, popes and the decorators of Hindu temples encouraged pregnancy and the spreading of the seed. It became a matter of personal pride throughout human society to create future generations to "carry on." To be "the end of the line" has been regarded as a great tragedy. Political leaders encouraged their people to have babies. Both Communists and Nazis gave medals to mothers who had done their duty to the nation by producing babies. Canada also awards baby-bearing mothers with financial incentives in the form of baby bonuses or mother's allowance. It may not be cheaper by the dozen, but it certainly can be profitable. At the same time, Revenue Canada rewards productive (in conception terms) parents by allowing deductions from taxable income for each dependent child. The more children, the smaller the income that will be taxed.

The political reasons for encouraging population growth are obvious. More people mean greater armies and potentially greater economic power, though the latter has not always proved to be true. A large population means that in times of famine, pestilence and war

there would be more people left to rebuild and to ensure the survival
of the nation.

This logic is duplicated at the personal and family level. In agricul-
tural societies, and even in many industrialized societies, more children
mean more money. Having more children means another two hands
to work the fields, to tend the animals, to work in the factories or to beg
in the streets. It means extra income. In the modern social welfare
state, it means extra welfare or mother's allowance. It also means
additional tax deductions.

In times gone by, infant mortality was considerably higher than it is
today. It was a rare family that did not lose at least one child either in
infancy or later in childhood. The now "historic" diseases of polio,
rheumatic fever and tuberculosis caused large death tolls. Having
babies was the safest replacement insurance available.

Times have changed—at least in the developed countries. Women,
like men, now have career ambitions which must be balanced with
their desire for children. Many couples are not interested in being
parents. Of those who are, many plan to have their children at times
when their finances and the social and employment situation will be
most beneficial to themselves and their children. In the meantime,
however, none of these couples want to give up sex. They want sex
without children.

In any discussion of birth control, the moral, ethical and political
problems of it are always raised. Millions of dollars and people are
rallied to promote legislation supporting their causes and thwarting
those of their opponents. Birthright, Planned Parenthood, Right to
Life and many other organizations involving an amazingly high
number of Canadians are constantly pressuring Parliament. Each
opposing side on any of these issues is so powerful a lobby that
Parliament has been unable to form a definite policy. As long as
society is divided on birth control issues, so will be Parliament, and so
will be the law. Each side will claim that the views of the other side are
being forced upon them. One side will claim that their position is
supported by all that is moral and right. They will speak in the name of
humanity. The opposing side will also speak in the name of humanity,
and in the name of morality and righteousness and of personal liberty
and freedom. Some will accuse their opponents of slipping towards
the dictates of Naziism or Communism.

In the developing world the West has been accused of promoting family planning as a means of controlling the population, and of controlling the Third World. The West responds by accusing the Third World of irresponsibility, which will result in famine, that the West will be called upon to correct. On a world scale, the controversy is never-ending. On a Canadian scale, the situation is no less stable. Flare-ups on a local basis, around hospitals and abortion policy, and around schools and sex education, occur constantly from coast to coast. Members of Parliament usually try to lay low.

## Pills and Things

The most common way of reducing the risk of pregnancy while continuing to have intercourse is accomplished by using a "medical device" or "the pill." While the pill is of fairly recent vintage, devices such as the condom for men and the diaphragm for women are generations old. In the past, birth control was viewed with a great deal of suspicion. People feared that it would lead to sexual promiscuity and the moral decline of society and the nation. Ladies "in the know" knew what to do, but the "great unwashed" were kept in the dark. The law reflected this attitude, as is seen in legislation passed by Parliament.

The federal Food and Drugs Act boldly states in 3(3), "Except as authorized by regulation, no person shall advertise to the general public any contraceptive device or any drug manufactured, sold or represented for use in the prevention of conception." It is the accused who must prove his innocence. He must prove that he was authorized by the regulations to advertise. The Crown prosecutor merely has to convince the court that advertising took place, regardless of how and why.

The picture is not as bleak as it first appears. In fact the regulations, which can be changed at any time by the Governor in Council (that is, the federal cabinet), are very liberal. They allow almost all contraceptive drugs to be advertised. All contraceptive devices other than intrauterine devices (IUDs) may be advertised to the general public by any means other than by the distribution of samples of the devices door-to-door or through the mail.

The medical devices regulations under the Food and Drugs Act lay down the standards for condoms in Canada. The standards specify a minimum length of 16 centimeters, a bursting volume of not less than 25 liters and that condoms must not contain or release harmful substances. Every package must have an expiry date not later than five years from the date of manufacture. The regulations even give the civil service detailed instructions on how to test condoms according to scientific methods.

To insure that there is no misunderstanding as to what sort of device is being regulated, the regulations define "condom." It is a sheath or covering intended to be worn on the penis during coitus for the purpose of preventing conception or for reducing the risk of transmission of disease. The latter purpose is clear federal recognition that extramarital sex does occur and that the government will assist those who do it in avoiding the risks. (See Chapter Seven: *V.D.: The Wages of Sin.*)

Contraceptive drugs, popularly known as "the pill," are also regulated by the federal government, in the same way as all other drugs—as to safety and reliability. The fact that the government allows the pill on the market however, does not mean that it is 100 percent safe, nor that it is 100 percent guaranteed to prevent pregnancy.

It is now known that the pill carries with it some very serious risks, the most serious being that of stroke and blood clots. If the risks materialize, does the woman have any legal recourse? She can only take action against the manufacturer of the drug if there was negligence in the making of the drug or in advising doctors of the risks.

She can take action against her doctor, but only if he was negligent in advising her of the risks. Did she fully comprehend them? Did the doctor explain them in a way so that she could reasonably have been expected to appreciate their seriousness? Suppose she told the doctor she did not want to hear about the risks. Can she complain later, on the basis that her doctor should have told her anyway?

Many of these difficulties become particularly acute when teenagers want the pill. Despite the popular impression to the contrary, patients under the age of majority can consent to their own medical care without the consent of their parents if they are capable of understanding. The degree of comprehension of the risks, however, may vary greatly from child to child. Provincial legislation in British Columbia does put some restrictions on a child's consent. (See L. E. Rozovsky, *The Canadian Patient's Book of Rights,* Chapter Four.)

## Sterilization

After drugs and devices, is sterilization: the permanent form of preventing conception. Sterilization ranges from the simplest form of surgery in a doctor's office, that of vasectomy for men, to the more serious hospital procedures for women of tubal ligation or even hysterectomy. The law does not single out sterilization procedures for special consideration. There are, however, special problems.

The first is that of consent. The patient must be told in an understandable manner the nature and risks of the operation. The rule is that the doctor must tell the patient everything that a reasonable person in the patient's position would want to know, such as the risk of death or disability. The patient must be told of the risk of pregnancy, especially in the period immediately following the surgery. (See Chapter Five: *Wrongful Birth and Life.*)

The most difficult problem is that of sterilizing a person who is not capable of consenting. Attempts are often made to sterilize the mentally retarded rather than to try to control their sexual activity. At one time, British Columbia and Alberta had eugenic sterilization boards which were required to approve all sterilizations of the disabled. The boards were eventually disbanded for being reminiscent of the German "medical" experiments conducted during World War II.

If a disabled person has a guardian or if he or she is under the age of majority, which is either 18 or 19 depending on the province, the parent may be asked to consent. Some lawyers feel that the consent of a parent or guardian is not sufficient since their authority is limited to consenting to beneficial medical procedures. The sterilization of a retarded male is of no benefit to him. The answer, many lawyers believe, is to let the courts decide the matter. Even this becomes difficult in cases of the disabled who have no guardians to protect their interests. The entire matter creates a messy legal situation and should be clarified by provincial legislation.

The third problem concerns whether the husband must give his consent for his wife's sterilization, or the wife for her husband's. The husband has never by law needed his wife's permission to be sterilized. She has never had a right to a fertile husband; it was considered merely a privilege. Traditionally, however, the husband did have a right over the body of his wife, and anyone who interfered with her body was interfering with the husband's rights. In recent years, no court has been faced with the problem. Except in a few provinces, such as Quebec, which have passed legislation, the law is uncertain. While a consultation with both parties may be desirable, the commonly held legal view now is that the husband's consent to his wife's sterilization is not necessary. (See Chapter Five: *The Legal Cost of Sex.*)

# Legal Abortions in Canada

After drugs, devices and sterilization, the most controversial method of preventing children is abortion. Many people think of it as a contraceptive method, but it is really nothing of the sort. The termination of the pregnancy occurs long after conception, during the development of the baby.

No other medical procedure has caused so much controversy. In British Columbia, rival groups have fought in their attempts to take over hospital societies and thus either prevent abortions or allow them in the hospital. The essential purpose of a hospital—providing medical care—is often forgotten in the struggle. In Prince Edward Island, the community was divided over the issue long before the hospital in question was even constructed.

The basis of the debate in this country and also abroad is the conflict between morality and personal freedom. If one believes that human life (and the soul) begins at conception, any method used to destroy that life, after it is conceived, is murder. Some believe that human life begins only when the fetus is viable, which is around six months after conception. At that point it could live independently of its mother. The destruction of the fetus beyond this point would then be murder. The third position is that no life exists until the child is born. Therefore, the decision whether or not to continue the pregnancy should be made personally by the pregnant woman. Those taking this position feel that any infringement on the woman's right to do what she will with her own body is a violation of her liberty. In Canada, it is the first and last positions that are popular.

Foreigners examining these two positions and how the law responds would be very confused. They would see that the anti-abortionists are complaining that the law is too liberal and that it allows for "abortion on demand." In many hospitals in Canada, as many as 95 percent of the requests for abortions are granted. This is not, therefore, an "abortion on demand" situation, but does come close to it. There are also hospitals that allow a much smaller percentage of requests and a vast number of hospitals that do not offer abortion services at all. In communities with only one hospital, and that hospital has a "no abortion" policy, it is impossible to get a pregnancy terminated legally in that community. The law is the same throughout Canada, but at the same time it allows for a variance in practice from community to community.

There is no legal right to an abortion in Canada. The law does not treat it like other medical procedures. Anyone performing or attempting an abortion on a woman, whether or not she is pregnant, is subject to prosecution under section 251 of the Criminal Code and liable to imprisonment for life. Any pregnant woman who attempts an abortion on herself is subject to imprisonment for two years. (See L. E. Rozovsky, *The Canadian Patient's Book of Rights,* Chapter Ten.)

Parliament did not dare to decriminalize abortions. Pro-life voters would have launched a mighty campaign that would have cost a number of pro-abortion M.P.s their jobs. On the other hand, Parliament had to do something or the pro-abortion voters would have voted out the pro-life M.P.s, in spite of the fact that most Canadians probably took the usual position: They did not care.

The result was to leave abortions as a criminal offense and expand the old defense of the necessity of saving the mother's life. The problem in the past was that anyone who wanted to perform an abortion was never certain whether his or her actions fell within the exception where the patient's life was in danger. It was necessary to wait until a criminal charge was laid and then attempt to convince a judge that the pregnancy would have endangered the mother. Such uncertainty discouraged doctors from performing abortions, but not the backstreet "boys" from working on their kitchen tables.

The compromise made in 1969 satisfied no one. It set up a procedure which gave doctors a certificate stating in advance that if an abortion was performed on a particular woman it would not be a criminal offense. This amendment to the Criminal Code was intended to allow women to have abortions performed by doctors if certain conditions were met. It was also intended to take business away from the back streets. No one really knows how many backstreet abortions are still performed or whether the number decreased after the law was changed. What is clear is that thousands of abortions are now legally performed in Canada.

The exception which now allows an abortion to take place, applies if the following conditions are met: 1) a therapeutic abortion committee consisting of at least three doctors appointed by the hospital has determined that the continued pregnancy "would or would be likely to endanger (the woman's) life or health;" 2) the abortion takes place in either a hospital accredited by the Canadian Council on Hospital Accreditation or a hospital approved by the provincial minister of health to do abortions; and 3) the woman consents to the abortion.

The law on abortion is so loose, like most compromises, that it gives very little guidance to anyone. It allows a very open policy and a very strict policy to coexist. Parliament has thrown the matter back into the laps of the public and has said, "We have opened the door. Who goes through it and how is not our concern." While this may be regarded as rather cowardly fence sitting, it was designed to reflect divided popular opinion. This, surely, is what democracy is all about.

Because of the wording of Canada's abortion law there are many questions left unanswered. Among the issues left unresolved by the law are the following:

• No hospital is forced to have a therapeutic abortion committee without which abortions cannot be performed in that hospital.

• No doctor is required to perform an abortion on his or her patients even if the pregnancy would endanger the patient's life or health and the committee has approved it.

• No particular method of abortion is ok, nor are any prohibited, but if a doctor negligently injures a woman, she, or if she dies her family, can take legal action for compensation.

• An abortion can legally take place at any time during a pregnancy, but if it is performed after it is safe, any resulting injuries may be considered as negligence in a suit brought against the doctor, who might also be charged with criminal negligence under the Criminal Code.

• No procedure is laid down by the Criminal Code as to how an application to a committee is to be made, as to whether the woman or her lawyer may appear before the committee, or as to whether the committee or the woman can bring in outside experts.

• The Criminal Code requires no special qualifications for members of therapeutic abortion committees other than that they be doctors. There is no requirement that any of them be psychiatrists, gynecologists, or *even* women, although in practice, hospitals may make appointments on these bases.

• There is no requirement that doctors performing abortions have any particular qualifications, though hospitals may have such rules.

• The Criminal Code does not give women any right of appeal of the committee's decision and, because of the wording of the law, a court challenge would be difficult.

• The Code sets no time limit within which committees must reach decisions, nor does it stipulate that they must in fact make decisions.

• There is no definition of the phrase "endanger her life or health."

This is left to the discretion of each committee and so leads to differing results. Some committees may view social and economic situations and the "pregnancy blues" as endangering life or health, while others require scientific evidence of a severe physical problem. The law has imposed on the committees the task of examining certain facts and opinions and of interpreting the words of the law to determine whether the facts and opinions fit within those words. Ordinarily, only legally trained judges are given this job. Not one member of the committee is a lawyer. If one member had to be a lawyer, one wonders whether decisions reached would be different.

The controversy over abortions will never subside. Each side, carrying the respective banners of democracy and morality, will whip itself into hysteria. The issue is extremely serious regardless of one's point of view. Unfortunately, it is unlikely ever to be resolved.

Assuming that the abortion provisions of the Criminal Code remain as written, there are two questions that the law must address: (1) *Does the father of the unborn child have the right to prevent the therapeutic abortion from being performed?* At one time, a husband had to consent to any medical treatment on his wife. These days by practice, and in Quebec and Ontario by legislation, a married woman can consent to her own medical treatment. The unsolved question is whether this applies to abortions. No court and no legislature have made a definite ruling on this matter in Canada.

The argument in favor of the husband's right to veto his wife's decision is that he was a partner in the creation of the unborn child. When the child is born, the father will have the legal right along with his wife to have custody of the child. He will also have the legal duty to support, educate and protect the child from harm. Thus he should have the same rights and duties, which the mother cannot take from him, over the unborn child. These same arguments would apply in the case of an unmarried couple.

If the expectant mother and father were married, the arguments in favor of the father's right to prevent an abortion would be stronger. There are many historical and social reasons for marriage. Traditionally, at least, one of these reasons was reproduction. It might be argued that the husband has a right to children if they could be born and that the mother has no right to deprive him of those children. Whether such an argument would be accepted by Canadian courts remains unsettled. English and American courts have not accepted it, and in one American judgment, the court said that a husband does not have a right to a baby-bearing wife and therefore could not prevent her abortion.

The argument against the husband or father interfering in the abortion relates to the mother's right to health care. In Canada, all abortions are, at least according to law, therapeutic. They can only be performed if the doctors on the therapeutic abortion committee say that it is "medically" necessary; that is, necessary to prevent danger to the woman's life or health. Even though some may criticize the committees' opinions in many cases, according to the law, an abortion cannot be performed unless it is medically necessary or therapeutic. An elective abortion based simply on the mother's desire not to have the child without any medical consideration is not legally possible. Since the husband cannot deprive his wife of medically necessary care, it follows that he could not prevent her from having a therapeutic abortion.

The only court actions that have taken place in Canada concerning the husband's rights have been applications by fathers for court orders preventing abortions. On occasion these have been granted, but the circumstances were such that the parties usually arrived at an agreement anyway. A Nova Scotia family court judge on one occasion appointed a guardian to protect and represent an unborn child. However, since no doctor in this case would do the abortion despite the approval of the abortion committee, the guardian never had to take action.

To get the law clarified, what is needed is a law suit brought by a husband or father against a doctor and the mother for compensation as a result of a therapeutic abortion. This would force a determination of the question of whether the husband really has a legal right in the first place. (2) *Does the law endanger a woman's health or life?* It is pointed out by most medical specialists that induced abortions performed during the early stages of pregnancy are practically risk-free. The risks increase substantially as the time of birth draws nearer.

Under current Canadian law the following situation is typical: A woman may not even suspect pregnancy despite having missed a menstrual period. By the time she becomes suspicious and arranges to see her doctor, the pregnancy is well into the second month or even into the third month. Even if the woman initially wants an abortion, her physician, her family and friends or her clergyman may try to talk her out of it. The result is further delay. Her doctor may refuse to have anything to do with the matter. She may be referred to another doctor or, if her doctor will not arrange a referral, she may have to find another doctor on her own. She may have to travel to another community. An application must then be presented to the committee. A doctor who has the time and is willing to perform the abortion must be found. A hospital bed must be found too, since most Canadian hospitals will not allow abortions on an outpatient basis. The committee must arrange to meet. There may be delays in obtaining specialist opinions. Time may begin to run on and the second trimester may be entered before the woman finally has everything arranged. By this time, the chance of encountering difficulties during the abortion procedure has increased.

Canadian law is criticized because many women experience lengthy delays due to procedural requirements. The contrary argument is that without these built-in delays, many decisions might be made all too precipitately, and the woman may later be extremely sorry. The debate is never-ending.

## Can the Abortion Law be Beaten?

It would appear that the law on abortions is straightforward and cannot be beaten without the patient leaving the country to have the abortion. But this is not so. It can be beaten, as Dr. Morgentaler, a Montreal doctor, proved in the early 1970s. He showed the country that one could perform an abortion outside of a hospital without the approval of a therapeutic abortion committee. The answer, he found, was to be able to convince a jury that the abortion was necessary, and that it was necessary to break the law in order to perform it. Despite Dr. Morgentaler's success, private abortion clinics outside of hospitals are not prepared to take the risk of a prosecution to determine whether they are able to get around the law.

# 4 Children Without Sex

The old refrain says, "If we can put a man on the moon, why can't we find a cure for cancer, heart disease or infertility?" Thanks to the astronauts, there have been major medical achievements at least in the last category. Talk of test tube babies and artificial wombs seems as farfetched as putting men in space or on the moon appeared in 1960. At least one "test tube" baby is alive in England and medical research continues on synthetic wombs. Developments are going at such a fast rate that children conceived without sex may someday be more common than children created *with* sex!

Along with all the achievements in curing various forms of infertility have come a number of serious legal and ethical issues. Some of the difficulties include artificial insemination, sperm banking and test tube babies, while others focus on the process of cloning and "womb-leasing." In this chapter, many of the legal problems are discussed. The ethics of using donor sperm or of cloning are left aside for each person to resolve for himself or herself.

## Artificial Insemination

Artificial insemination is not a recent medical technique devised by scientists. The process was developed around 1322 when a group of Arabian gentlemen impregnated the mares of their enemy with semen from inferior stallions. In the 17th and 18th centuries, artificial insemination was used to fertilize fish eggs and to impregnate an insect, a dog and an amphibian. The first reported case of artificial insemination involving human beings occurred in England in 1799. In that case, semen was withdrawn from the husband by means of a syringe and then injected into his wife's uterus. The first reported case of artificial insemination using donor sperm occurred in 1884, when semen from a medical student was used to impregnate a married woman whose husband was sterile. Today, thousands of children throughout North America are conceived by means of artificial insemination using sperm collected from husbands and donors alike.

## Artificial Insemination Procedures

The collection of semen for artificial insemination is a relatively easy procedure. When taken from the husband, it usually is referred to as A.I.H. (Artificial Insemination Husband) and when given by a donor, A.I.D. (Artificial Insemination Donor). Sperm is usually taken from the husband to impregnate his wife when there is a physical impediment which prevents conception through normal sexual intercourse. Donor sperm is used when the husband's sperm count is too low or the sperm lacks sufficient spontaneous movement to ensure passage to the woman's ovum or egg which awaits fertilization. Donor sperm is also used if there is any genetic disorder which the husband carries that could affect the offspring. This would include certain types of muscular dystrophy and Tay-Sachs disease.

Sperm collection involves masturbation into a container within two hours of the time set for the insemination procedure. Sperm may also be taken from a sperm bank where it has been frozen under carefully controlled conditions. Where the husband's condition is one of low-sperm count, some of his sperm may be mixed with that of a selected donor.

The sperm is injected into the woman's cervix and upper vagina one or two days prior to ovulation. Injections are continued at intervals of two days throughout the woman's fertile phase. This is usually determined by monitoring the woman's body temperature. Once the sperm has been injected, the woman must remain in the treatment position for about 30 minutes. A packing material is then inserted and left in place for eight hours. Another method involves a "cervical cup" which is inserted into the cervix. The semen is injected into a pump-like device located in the cup and left for four hours. The sperm, in either method, is left to "do its thing" and fertilize the egg. The success rate using donor sperm is usually around 80 to 85 percent.

## Selection of Donors

There are a number of psychological and emotional problems experienced by many men who find they cannot father their own child. It may be a matter of feeling frustrated or inadequate. It can lead to a strain in the marriage or even marital break up. Recognizing this, fertility physicians have set a number of guidelines to follow in using donor sperm. All attempts to impregnate the wife through intercourse or through artificial insemination using the husband's sperm must have been exhausted. The only exception is if the husband has been identified as a carrier of a known genetic disorder.

Once the couple decide to use donated (or purchased) sperm, the fertility specialist tries to obtain sperm from a good "match." This means a male who, within reasonable limits, has the same physical characteristics, ethnic background and blood type as the husband. Donors are usually screened to make sure that they are not carriers of a genetic disorder. Some specialists restrict the potential pool of donors to men who themselves have fathered healthy children. They must undergo successful semen analysis and provide details of family history which indicate they are not carriers of some familial disease trait. Often, the donors are medical personnel who work in or study at the medical school or center where the fertility work takes place. The same donor may be used on a number of occasions. In each instance the identity of the donor and the recipient is kept confidential.

## Sperm Banks

Sperm banking is part of the overall artificial insemination process. Human sperm banking got quite a push in the early 1960s when scientists became concerned about the effects of radiation in space on the sperm of astronauts. Methods were developed to freeze and store their sperm, so that they could still have children after their return to earth, even if their semen was destroyed or damaged. Further developments in sperm banking occurred during the Vietnam war. Scientists realized that many soldiers would be killed or injured in such a way that they could no longer engage in sexual intercourse or produce children. Sperm banking offered them an opportunity to have children regardless of their injuries.

Today, sperm banks can be found throughout the world. The semen of donors is frozen and stored for use at a later time. The sperm is coded to assure anonymity. Characteristics of the donor, including race or ethnic background, eye color, hair color and blood type are noted for matching purposes.

The medical issues in choosing candidates for artificial insemination, the use of donor sperm and sperm banking are often overshadowed by legal problems. Some of the legal issues can be quickly resolved, whereas others may not have any legal solutions.

## Legal Considerations of Artificial Insemination

Most of the legal problems in artificial insemination involve the use of donor sperm. Such matters as consent and from whom, adultery, illegitimacy, defective sperm and defective offspring, custody, confidentiality and child support are only some of the legal concerns. New ones have also appeared, such as the right of a widow, a divorcée or a single woman to have artificial insemination. Throughout the world, courts, legislatures, physicians and theologians have attempted to resolve these matters. In Canada, many of these concerns have not been resolved by provincial assemblies or the courts. In most instances, Canadians have decided what should be done between themselves and their physicians. This method of problem solving may be good for a few, but it leaves unanswered a number of questions for many more Canadians.

## Consent, Adultery, Illegitimacy and Artificial Insemination Consent

Although it is now well established in Canadian law that a woman need not secure permission from her husband for medical treatment, artificial insemination may be an exception to that rule. Since the mother's husband will likely have to provide support for a child conceived by means of artificial insemination, it is argued that at least he should have a voice in the decision. If the wife were to go ahead with insemination using donor sperm without her husband's agreement, it could constitute grounds for divorce. The husband may be so grievously hurt and emotionally distraught that, in filing for divorce, he might win on the ground of mental cruelty. More likely, however, would be a charge of adultery. In fact, whether or not the husband gives his permission to the use of donor sperm, it is possible that he could file charges of adultery.

As a matter of procedure, most fertility specialists and fertility clinics require that both the wife *and* the husband sign a consent form to the use of donor sperm. This decision is the culmination of long discussions with physicians following the failure of attempts at using the husband's healthy sperm (if there are any). Consent, however, may not be enough to protect the doctor, the donor or the wife from a variety of legal allegations.

## Adultery

In 1913, Mr. and Mrs. Orford were married in Canada. They spent the next several months honeymooning in Europe. Thereafter, the couple split up. The wife returned to England and the husband to Canada. Their marriage had not been consummated due to a physical problem experienced by the wife. In 1919, the wife gave birth to a child, allegedly having become pregnant through artificial insemination. The husband had not consented to it nor did he have any knowledge of it. In the subsequent divorce suit, Mr. Orford accused his wife of committing adultery. Her lawyer argued that artificial insemination was *not* adultery, since it did not include sexual intercourse. The court agreed with Mr. Orford, saying that adultery includes sexual intercourse *or* any "voluntary surrender to another person of the reproductive powers or faculties of the guilty person." This decision continues to puzzle legal authorities, since it does not meet the traditional Common Law definition of adultery, which includes the penetration of a woman by a man.

As no other decision has been handed down in Canada, the law is unclear on the status of artificial insemination as an act of adultery. There is no legislation in Canada which specifically condones or condemns artificial insemination. Under the Divorce Act, artificial insemination is not listed as a basis for adultery. In a number of American states, artificial insemination using a donor's sperm has been legalized as long as the consent of both the husband and wife has been secured. Many of these laws require that a licensed physician perform the insemination procedure. The statutes also specify that, in the eyes of the law, the husband and *not* the donor is to be treated as the father of the child. It has been argued that Canada should have similar laws recognizing artificial insemination and the legal consequences of it.

## Legitimacy, Child Support and Inheritance

The concern about adultery has far-reaching implications. If the artificial insemination is considered adulterous, any child conceived in this way would be considered illegitimate. An illegitimate child may not be entitled to child support from his mother's husband and could possibly be denied the right of inheritance from his "father." Fortunately, reforms in legislation controlling family law and long-standing principles in the Common Law have had the effect of reducing greatly the legitimacy-illegitimacy distinction in artificial insemination.

According to Common Law, a child born during a marital relationship is presumed to be the legitimate offspring of the couple. The burden is on the contesting party to prove that the husband did not father the child. To say that the child and the husband have the same blood type does not prove that the husband is or is not the father. More sophisticated scientific evidence may be necessary, including the testing of blood subgroups or even genetic tests.

Even if a child is considered illegitimate, the husband may not escape responsibility for child support and maintenance. There are a number of provincial statutes which have gone far beyond the Common Law presumption of legitimacy. Ontario, in its Family Law Reform Act, defines a "child" as a person either born within or outside the marriage. It also includes an individual towards whom the parent has shown an intention to treat as part of the family. Nova Scotia, in its Children's Maintenance Act, designates that a guardian must provide for the necessities of life for any child in his or her household 16 years of age or younger. "Guardian," in this context, includes any person who is the head of a household or who has custody or control of a child. Under either form of legislation, the fact that the husband may not have fathered the child does not remove his responsibility of child support and maintenance.

The question arises as to whether the donor of the sperm would escape financial responsibility for the child. It may be difficult to identify the donor, since the physician or sperm bank who obtained the sperm maintain strict rules of confidentiality and may refuse to disclose the donor's identity. The task may be even more difficult if the sperm was "imported" from a sperm bank outside Canada. The sperm of several donors may also have been mixed in the insemination. The sperm may have been deposited long before insemination or the donor may have moved or died. Even if the identity of the donor were known, it may be impossible or at least difficult to trace him.

Legislation creating a presumption that a child born during a marriage is the child of that couple may exclude the donor as a source of support since he is presumed not to be the father. The laws governing child support and maintenance are more concerned with the broad aspects of child custody and control than with who is, or may be, the biological father. The fact that a husband consented to the artificial insemination does not make the child legitimate, but it is a matter that the court would consider in pinning financial responsibility.

The law, therefore, would tend to look at how a husband and wife act toward a child born during their marriage rather than at the child's genetic makeup. It is much more likely that the "father" and not the donor would be turned to as a source of financial support.

## Inheritance

Artificial insemination can also affect a child's right of inheritance. In Common Law, an illegitimate child could not inherit from his mother's husband even though the child might have viewed him as his "father." In the United States, courts have ruled that many of the old legal distinctions between legitimate and illegitimate children in matters of inheritance must be removed. The right of inheritance has been affected by these court rulings so that illegitimate children can obtain a share of their parent's estate. In Canada, provincial legislation has begun to have the same effect. Ontario has eliminated the illegitimate-legitimate distinction, treating all children on an equal basis. For example, a husband angered by his wife's artificial insemination obtained without his consent may attempt to "cut off" the child in his will. Under Ontario law, however, if the child can prove that while the "father" was alive he demonstrated an intention to consider the child part of the family, a court may act to provide the child with a share of the estate. This is not to say that the child would be successful in all cases, since evidence may be revealed that shows that he was left out for some reason other than the way he was conceived.

## Responsibility of the Physician and Sperm Bank in Artificial Insemination

In any medical situation, a physician must act in a reasonable and prudent manner towards his patients. He must provide care in a fashion that is consistent with average, reasonable standards, derived from the experience of the medical community. When a physician fails to meet this standard and reasonably foreseeable consequent injury results, the physician is considered negligent and must compensate the patient for the injury. Similarly, a sperm bank is expected to meet the minimum reasonable standards of operation and management of institutions engaged in the collection, storage and distribution of sperm.

Failure to properly test the semen by accepted methods could be considered negligence if the woman does not become pregnant or suffers a miscarriage. The donor's sperm may have been as problematic as that of the husband; it may have some defect, or, in the case of sperm taken from a sperm bank, it may not have been stored properly.

A few more interesting problems may arise from improper matching. Since the semen taken from a sperm bank is usually coded to maintain donor anonymity, it is possible for sperm to be mislabeled. Thus a couple of Italian or Greek heritage thinking that the donor was of the same ethnic extraction could end up with a child who is partly black or Chinese. The parents may be so emotionally distraught that they wish to sue the doctor and the sperm bank. It is then obvious that the husband is not the father. The doctor may be partly responsible for not double-checking the sperm bank's analysis, and the sperm bank, in turn, may have been negligent in its labeling procedures. The fact that some negligence occurred does not necessarily mean the parents would win an award of money damages. Courts only award damages if someone has been injured.

In Canada, money damages may be awarded for nervous shock, but the situations in which the courts have responded are limited to exceptionally horrible occurrences. It is doubtful that a husband and wife, upon learning that their child conceived through artificial insemination was not of the "correct" race, would experience such severe emotional shock as to result in life-long mental damage. In this case, the parents are faced with a healthy child, although one not of their desired ethnic background. Courts would likely make short shrift of a request for money damages in this circumstance.

An entirely different outcome may result if the child, born by way of donated sperm, is afflicted with birth or genetic defects. If it can be shown that the doctor or the sperm bank negligently failed to detect a lethal or defective trait in the donor's sperm and the child was born with it, a successful lawsuit may follow.

One instance in which this might occur could involve Jewish people of Eastern European stock. Many of the descendants from this part of the world are carriers of a fatal ailment called Tay-Sachs disease which is passed on to newborns. Although the child at birth appears normal, he rapidly deteriorates and usually dies before the age of four or five.

Couples who are carriers of Tay-Sachs are sometimes advised to have children using donated sperm. A tragic irony would be for such a couple to receive sperm that was incorrectly screened as being negative for Tay-Sachs. There are no reports of any Canadian court ruling on such a case. It would appear, however, that if negligence could be proven against the doctor and the sperm bank, both would be liable for the expenses incurred in raising the child and perhaps for his wrongful death. (For further discussion of damages see Chapter Five: *Wrongful Birth and Life* and Chapter Six: *The Legal Cost of Sex*.)

Donor-recipient confidentiality is another area of responsibility for physicians and sperm banks. Since the idea behind donor artificial insemination is to produce a child who will be viewed as the offspring of a marriage, attempts at identifying the biological "father" are discouraged. Donors may become curious about the offspring they have produced. A child finding out that another man fathered him may be interested in background information about him. Short of a court order or statute compelling disclosure of details regarding the donor or the recipient, no physician or sperm bank will reveal confidential information. In most instances, prior to the insemination procedure, both the recipient and her husband and the donor and his wife are required to sign a legal document in which they give up certain rights. Among the rights relinquished by the donor are the opportunity of knowing who got the semen, and visitation rights with the child born of that sperm. The recipient loses the right to receive details regarding who gave the sperm. There is also an agreement that the donor will not be responsible for the child's support and maintenance.

Should a physician or sperm bank disclose confidential information about either any women impregnated with donor sperm or any donor, legal consequences might arise. However, the person harmed by this breach of confidentiality would have to prove that the disclosure was not authorized and that he or she has been harmed by it.

With the absence of legislation or regulations governing artificial insemination, physicians and sperm banks have been left to themselves to develop criteria for the collection, storage and use of sperm. Prior to recommending artificial insemination, most people go through careful examination and selection. Even if all procedures are followed, however, errors, breaches of confidentiality and negligence can occur.

Some situations are far beyond the control of the sperm banks, such as the marriage of two people born of artificial insemination with sperm from the same donor. Under most provincial statutes such a marriage between a half brother and a half sister is illegal. How could the couple know about their common origin? Should the doctor or the sperm bank be held accountable for such a twist of fate? Doctors and sperm banks carry a tremendous responsibility. The language of the legal documents signed by the parties, which are designed to relieve them of some of this responsibility, may not be totally effective. They are still accountable for negligence, and therefore, must be diligent in their far-reaching activities.

## Artificial Insemination and the Single Woman

A grave concern facing fertility specialists is whether they may legally impregnate a single woman by artificial insemination. There have not been any reported Canadian cases on the issue, nor is there any legislation in Canada which either approves or prohibits it. This presents an interesting legal problem since it involves many moral and ethical considerations.

For a physician to knowingly impregnate a single woman by artificial insemination could lead to charges of unprofessional conduct and the suspension or revocation of his license. He would be participating in the conception of an illegitimate child, one who might ultimately become a financial burden to the community.

From the woman's perspective, this might appear as utter nonsense. Ontario, as noted earlier, has set the pace in abolishing the distinctions between legitimacy and illegitimacy. Other provinces may follow. Fears that a child born to a single parent may become a welfare case are pure speculation. The woman may even raise the banner of unfair discrimination between persons of her status and women who are married. She would argue that since single parents may now adopt children, there should not be any distinction in marital status drawn in terms of artificial insemination.

Unlike the situation in Canada, there has been one court case in the United States. A young single New Jersey woman wanted to be inseminated with sperm donated by a male friend. Doctors who received the request declined to perform the procedure because of her single status. The woman and her friend, however, did obtain instructions from a sperm bank as to the means of achieving artificial insemination. Following regular trips to her friend's apartment during which she inseminated herself artificially with his sperm, she became pregnant. The matter went to court when she denied her friend visitation rights with "their" child. The court decided that the father did have the right to visit with his child and the duty to provide financial support. The judge declared that this was the least that could be done to lessen the impact of illegitimacy upon the child while providing him with some sense of family association.

In many American states, legislation prohibits the carrying out of artificial insemination by anyone other than a licensed physician. The law also requires the consent of the wife and her husband, thus eliminating the prospect of single women receiving medically administered insemination. It is possible, under these laws, that a person who performs self-insemination or aids an unlicensed person would be subject to charges of the illegal practice of medicine.

Although some may sympathize with the wishes of the single woman, one cannot overlook the needs and rights of her potential offspring. Laws may abolish illegitimacy as a legal status, but the social stigma will linger on for quite some time. Government has the responsibility of promoting and protecting the best interests of all children inadequately provided for by their parents. Single parent insemination is one area in which governments may act to prevent problems before they occur. Prohibiting artificial insemination for unmarried women, or setting stringent guidelines which allow it only on a case-by-case basis, would go a long way to protect the best interests of the children.

## "Test Tube" Babies

Ever since the birth of Louise Brown a few years ago in England, there has been a tremendous amount of discussion about "test tube" babies. Many people have a mental image of human fetuses literally growing in huge test tubes. What is really meant by "test tube" babies is quite different. The process also has some important legal considerations.

### What are "Test Tube" Babies?

Until the last several years, if a woman for one reason or another could not conceive, she and her husband had no alternative but to adopt. In at least one type of infertility problem, this is no longer the case.

A woman with damaged fallopian tubes, the vessels through which the egg is transported to the uterus, may be a candidate for reimplantation of an egg removed from, and fertilized outside, her body. The procedure, simply described, is this. When it is determined that the woman is ovulating, the egg or ovum is removed by surgery. The egg is then incubated in a chemical solution mixed with sperm for 12 to 18 hours. Once the egg has been fertilized and it has grown sufficiently, it is reimplanted in the woman's body. Growth continues in the usual manner.

Despite sophisticated methods of collecting the husband's sperm and implantation of the fertilized egg, there have been only a few reported successful births of "test tube" babies. More research on the process is necessary to standardize this method of conception.

## Legal Consequences of "Test Tube" Conceptions

As the number of artificial methods of conception increase, there will be new legal and ethical concerns over the consequences of this technology. Much of the ethical debate will never be resolved. From a legal viewpoint, however, there is at least one key issue.

If the physician who performs the test tube fertilization procedure does so improperly and causes injury, he can be sued for negligence, just as the errant surgeon is held accountable for faulty surgery. It may be a matter of implanting the fertilized egg at the wrong time, inserting it in a negligent manner or taking some incorrect step in the fertilization process. As long as the woman or husband can prove that the doctor failed to measure up to a reasonable standard of care and as a result reasonably foreseeable injury occurred, the physician may be held negligent. As with other experimental or novel procedures which are risky, test tube fertilization, in the eyes of the law, may require the doctor to meet a higher than usual standard of care. A person carrying out new or dangerous procedures must be particularly diligent.

Physicians engaged in test tube conception are not the only people who may be held negligent. The laboratory, which tests the husband's sperm and collects it for fertilization, could be held negligent if the tests are improperly conducted or the sperm improperly handled. If, for example, the test results indicate the husband is not a carrier of a dreaded disease, when in fact he is and a deformed child results, it is possible that a negligence verdict would result. Similarly, if the sperm is not properly stored or handled so that it is damaged and conception is impossible, the laboratory and its employees may be held accountable.

The test tube conception process is still quite new. In legal terms, this means that untested, novel legal theories remain on the horizon. This may include "wrongful life" cases where the test tube child born with a defect sues the physician or even his parents for being born.

(See Chapter Five: *Wrongful Birth and Life.*) At present, however, physicians involved in test tube fertilization must be diligent when carrying out the process. Couples considering the possibility of raising a family in this way should make certain they understand the process, including all the known risks and the likelihood of successful conceptions. Test tube pregnancies remain a novel aspect of children without sex.

## The Law of Rent-a-Womb

For some women pregnancy is totally impossible. Even the test tube fertilization process is unworkable because they are unable to give birth. This may be due to disease, hysterectomy, or genetic defects which might be passed on to any offspring. For other women, it is a matter of convenience. They want children but they do not want the nine months of pregnancy. Whatever the reason, they still want children fathered by their husbands. The question is, who will carry the child for the duration of the pregnancy? What are the legal consequences of the solution of "rent-a-womb"?

## The "Rent-a-Womb" Concept

There are three different situations in which womb-renting might occur. First, it might be used by women who can conceive, but for whom pregnancy could be dangerous or fatal. In each case, the woman's egg is fertilized, either in her, or outside her, by the test tube method. It is then implanted in the uterus of another woman who carries the child until birth. While this may be done as a personal favor, it is more likely done for money. At birth the child is turned over to his biological or genetic parents.

The second group to whom womb-renting is appealing are those women who want children but who, for convenience, do not want to go through conception or pregnancy. It requires an arrangement with another woman to become pregnant by artificial insemination with the sperm of the would-be mother's husband and then to carry the child to birth. The child is then given to his "parents." The couple usually pays the "surrogate" mother a fee for her services.

The third group who would take advantage of the procedure are those women who physically can neither conceive on their own nor carry to birth a child conceived by artificial insemination. Women who have undergone surgical removal of their ovaries or who have had hysterectomies would be in this category. Their children would be conceived and born in the same way as those of women in the second group who use "surrogate" mothers for convenience. Another woman would agree to becoming pregnant through artificial insemination with the husband's sperm. She would "rent out" her womb for the duration of pregnancy and at birth give the child to his parents. The procedure is not too different from hiring a vehicle from a rent-a-car agency.

## The Legal Consequences

There are a variety of legal issues that are raised by womb-leasing arrangements. Some may involve the surrogate mother, while others may involve the "parents." Many issues have never been presented to courts or legislators for resolution.

(1) *Negligence.* The physician or other person who arranged for the services of the surrogate parent may be held negligent if they select a woman who passes on a defect or disease to the fetus. The situation could arise if the surrogate was not checked properly for genetic defects or diseases such as gonorrhea. It could also arise if the fertilized egg of the mother is implanted in a surrogate who is not biologically compatible. If the surrogate knew or ought to have known she was not a suitable person for the task, and as a result the child is miscarried or born damaged, it is possible that she too could be held negligent.

(2) *Custody and Breach of Contract.* It is possible that the surrogate mother may become so attached to the child she bore that she changes her mind and refuses to surrender the child to his "parents." The problem could become even more complex if the surrogate is the biological mother of the infant, that is, the egg was not transplanted from the wife but was produced by the surrogate's body. If the surrogate is the child's real mother, why should she be forced to give him up?

Enterprising lawyers in the womb-leasing field are certain to require written contracts between the "parents" and the surrogate. It would likely contain language that either empowers a court to compel the surrogate to give the child to his "parents" at birth, or recognizes that at birth the child in the eyes of the law is considered the product of the "parent's" marriage.

There is also the possibility of breach of contract, which could nullify the contract. If there is a schedule of payments to the surrogate and the couple fail to make these sums available, there would be a breach of the contract. Similarly, if the couple were required to make provision for the surrogate's accommodation and maternity needs and they failed to do so, it would be a breach of the contract. In the case of the parents failing to meet the contractual arrangements, could the surrogate insist on keeping the child? Would she be justified in having an abortion? Would a court award her custody on this basis? Could she demand that the biological father provide child support? Could the "parents" in return demand visiting privileges? Can the parents sue the surrogate if she fails to look after herself properly, or has an abortion? Is this a breach of contract?

Courts in Canada have not been faced with these questions. It is unlikely, however, that the failure to make contractual payments or to provide accommodation would be enough for a court to award custody to the surrogate. A womb-leasing agreement is not like a leasing arrangement for a car or a piece of equipment. Breach of property leases can be resolved by money damages. Custody of a "womb-leasing child" is quite another matter. Courts presented with such cases in the future will have quite a dilemma to resolve. At the moment, we can only speculate as to the outcome and look to developing trends in the United States.

In California an actual legal challenge has arisen involving the rent-a-womb concept. A 29-year-old California widow agreed to become inseminated artificially with the sperm of a New York man, James Noyes. Mr. Noyes and his wife were unable to have children of their own because Mrs. Noyes was a hermaphrodite. The California woman, Nisa Bhimani, promised to carry to term any child conceived with the sperm and to give up any parental rights she might have in favor of Mr. and Mrs. Noyes. Sometime during her pregnancy the surrogate mother changed her mind and she informed the "parents" that she had decided to keep the child.

A custody battle followed in the California courts. After a closed hearing, however, the custody claim was dropped at least for the time being. A lawyer representing Mr. and Mrs. Noyes suggested that they had decided not to press the matter since they felt such a decision was in the child's best interest. In any event, to complicate the child's status, the court ordered that Mrs. Bhimani retain custody but that Mr. Noyes be named the father on the child's birth certificate. At the very least the case illustrates how awkward and complex it can be to rent-a-womb.

## The Future of Children Without Sex

On the medical horizon, there are fascinating and provocative technical advances which will likely increase the number of children produced without sex. Some will be born of artificial wombs, mechanical devices which approximate the environment of the womb. Others will be "cloned." Cloning, the asexual reproduction of cells from one parent, means that virtually countless "carbon copies" of the same person could be produced. From this process, armies of strong, robust soldiers, groups of extremely intelligent scientists, and meek, subservient workers could be produced. The legal and moral prospects of cloning are only speculative now, as is the possibility of artificial wombs. So, too, were test tube babies a few years ago. Society must begin to consider these future prospects, and if and how the production of children without sex is to be regulated. Children born of sexual intercourse may otherwise become quite *passé*.

# 5 Wrongful Birth and Life

"Oops! I'm pregnant," she says. "Not again!" he replies. How many millions of times has this happened? How many Canadians are "accidents?" The "gift of life" bestowed accidentally on shocked mothers and fathers may cause marital strains and disruption of family life, as well as providing gossip for neighbors, and friends who have been "careful." Regardless of the social consequences and of husbands and wives blaming each other, the law is seldom involved.

The legal problems arise not from accidental births but from "wrongful" births caused by a third party. The questions then arise as to who can sue whom, for what wrongful acts and for how much. The situations in which legal solutions are sought generally involve either negligence or rape.

## The Questions

There are at least eight situations in which someone, other than the parents, can cause what the law calls a wrongful birth or a wrongful life.

• A physician performs a sterilization on a woman. He does not use the proper techniques in tying her fallopian tubes and as a result she is still fertile and becomes pregnant. A physician performs a vasectomy. He fails to advise his patient that for several weeks he may continue to be fertile. The man, believing he is sterile, takes no precautions and in short order he is a "wrongful father." Is the physician in either case responsible for the unwanted pregnancy? For the wrongful birth? For the bringing up of the child? Is the physician responsible only to the patient upon whom he performed the sterilization, or to the patient's spouse as well? Does he, in addition, have a responsibility to the child?

• A physician advises a woman or a man that they are unable to parent. As a result, the patient ceases to use birth control methods and a wrongful birth results. Is the physician responsible?

• A physician fails to advise a woman that she has a high risk of giving birth to a deformed child. She takes no precautions and a deformed child is born or the woman may already be pregnant. Her doctor knows, or ought to know, that she is carrying a deformed child. He fails to have the necessary tests carried out to confirm his suspicions and the birth takes place. If the woman knew the truth she may have applied for a therapeutic abortion. Is the doctor responsible for the birth of a deformed child? If so, to what extent?

• A woman gets a prescription for birth control pills. Her druggist gives her vitamin pills by mistake. She becomes very healthy—and very pregnant. Is the pharmacist responsible? If the doctor made the prescription error is he legally responsible?

• A man purchases a condom. There is a defect in it. His partner becomes pregnant. There is a defect in a diaphragm and the woman becomes pregnant. The manufacture of "the pill" is imperfect and pregnancy results. In all of these cases, is the manufacturer responsible?

• A physician performs a sterilization procedure on a man or a woman, but unlike in the first case, guarantees the patient that he or she no longer needs to worry about having children. If, subsequently, the man fathers a child or the woman gives birth to a baby, can the physician be sued for breach of contract? Is the doctor's assurance and verbal guarantee enough to create a contract?

• A surgeon improperly performs surgery causing a woman to give birth to a deformed child. The woman is not injured and the surgery took place long before the birth. Is the surgeon responsible to the woman? To the child?

• A man rapes a married woman and she becomes pregnant. He is convicted and sent to prison, only to be released on probation after a few years. The woman is a Roman Catholic and would not have an abortion. The rapist has paid his debt to society, but what about a debt to the woman for the rape? For the pregnancy? For the child? Does the woman's husband have a claim against the rapist? If he does, what is it for? Does the husband have any responsibility for the support of the child? Does it make any difference if the woman is single?

## What is Negligence?

To discover the answers to all of these questions, one cannot look in the statute books. Provincial and federal acts and regulations will be of no help. The answer is to be found in the English Common Law of negligence in all provinces except Quebec, and in that province, in the Civil Code.

According to law, every person suing another, whether he is suing a doctor, pharmacist or manufacturer, owes a duty of care to those who may be affected by his actions. This duty is to exercise his service with, as was stated in an 1838 British case, "a reasonable degree of care and skill." He must act as the average, reasonable and prudent doctor, pharmacist or manufacturer would act in the circumstances. There is no duty to be perfect, or to never make an error; only to be reasonable.

What is reasonable depends on the profession or expertise that is being offered. The specialist is held to a higher standard than the general practitioner. It also depends on the circumstances. A physician is not required to abide by all proper standards of hygiene in an emergency when the time required to carry out these standards would further endanger the patient. Because the work of a physician particularly, and in some instances that of a pharmacist, involves judgment, errors will naturally occur from time to time. Some of these errors may injure and even kill patients. There is no legal right for the patient or his family to seek compensation from the person who made the error in judgment as long as average, reasonable and prudent standards were followed in making that judgment. Even if these standards were not followed, no action can be taken if there was no injury, or if the injury was not reasonably foreseeable.

Negligence is the failure of a person to abide by the average, reasonable, prudent standards of that person's profession or expertise *and* as a result cause reasonably foreseeable injury. The victim of negligence, in order to be compensated, must prove both parts of the equation. This principle can be applied to any situation: to the lawyer who makes a mess of a real estate title search, to the garage mechanic who fails to tighten bolts which results in an accident, to the physician who gives improper advice, to the pharmacist who dispenses the wrong drug and to the manufacturer who produces a defective, dangerous product. Similarly, it can be applied to what are known as the wrongful birth and wrongful life cases.

"Wrongful birth" is a legal action brought by one or both parents claiming injury due to the birth of a child as a result of the negligence of the defendant, that is the person being sued. "Wrongful life" is an action brought by the child alleging that he or she should not have been born and that being alive is an injury.

Both of these cases must be examined in two situations. The first is the suit brought for wrongful birth or life even though the child is normal and healthy. The injury here is the birth and the fact that the child exists at all. The second situation arises when the child is deformed or otherwise abnormal. The question is raised whether the law relating to the birth of an abnormal child should be different from that of a normal child.

## Breach of Contract and Wrongful Life

Legal actions may also be brought on the basis that there was a contract between the mother and the defendant that the mother would not become pregnant. Breach of contract lawsuits do not require proof of negligence. A sterilization procedure could be performed without negligence, but the doctor could be sued for breach of contract if he promised or guaranteed that the patient would no longer bear children. In both Canada and the United States, physicians have been held responsible in breach of contract cases when they have guaranteed certain results. Many of the cases have involved plastic or cosmetic surgery. Although there have been no reported cases of breach of contract cases involving unwanted pregnancies, the same principle would apply. Guaranteeing the results of a vasectomy or a procedure which leaves a woman sterile could cost the doctor a lot in the long run if a child is born to the supposedly "sterile" couple.

## Can the Mother Sue for Wrongful Birth of a Healthy Child?

By the end of 1980, there had only been four reported Canadian lawsuits dealing with either wrongful birth, wrongful pregnancy or wrongful life. One case occurred in Quebec, another in Ontario and two more in Alberta.

In the Alberta cases, both against the same doctor, one was successful, the other not. In the first case in 1977, the physician attempted to sterilize a woman in his office using an experimental technique. He did not tell her that the procedure was experimental, nor that there would still be a risk of pregnancy. Even after he knew that the sterilization had not been successful, he failed to inform the patient. She could have used other contraceptive methods but, thinking that she was sterile, she did not bother. She became pregnant and required an abortion and hysterectomy. She sued for wrongful pregnancy and won.

In the second case reported in 1979, the physician had informed the woman of the nature and risks of the sterilization procedure, the same procedure used in the earlier case. He did not imply nor give any guarantee of success. He had carried out the sterilization according to all reasonable and prudent standards. Unfortunately, the sterilization was unsuccessful and this patient also became pregnant. She sued and lost. It was not the doctor's fault and there had been no implied "contract" or guarantee of sterilization.

An Ontario doctor also won a case brought against him for an unsuccessful sterilization. He used an average, reasonable and prudent technique even though many physicians said they would not have used it. As in the Alberta doctor's second case, the physician told the patient that there was still a risk of pregnancy. Thus there was no case to be made for wrongful pregnancy.

The most complex of all the cases was that of *Cataford* v. *Moreau,* which was decided by the Chief Justice of the Quebec Superior Court on June 1, 1978.

Mrs. Cataford was an English speaking Indian from the Oka Reserve. Her husband was French speaking and, for all practical purposes, illiterate. He had been out working since he was nine. The couple was married at Oka on February 11, 1957. The groom was 26; the bride 19. On March 31, 1968 Mrs. Cataford gave birth to their tenth child. All ten survived and lived at home.

Mrs. Cataford then began to use birth control pills, but had to give them up after several years because she could not tolerate the side effects. Her family physician referred her to Dr. Antonio Moreau, a surgeon.

On August 24, 1971 Mrs. Cataford was admitted to hospital. She and her husband were asked to sign a form marked "Sterilization Request." The Chief Justice placed no importance on the form since: 1) the husband, being French speaking and illiterate was incapable of understanding the form, which was in English, and no one explained it to him; 2) the wife, being English speaking and poorly educated, signed the form without reading it and could not have read the section about surgery, as it had been added in French; 3) the form, even if it had been understood, stated that there would be no possibility to conceive.

Dr. Moreau performed the sterilization, a tubal ligation, on August 25, 1971. On September 15, 1972 Mrs. Cataford gave birth to her 11th child, Marcel, a healthy boy. Mr. and Mrs. Cataford sued Dr. Moreau on the basis of medical negligence and wrongful birth. The court found that the sterilization was performed negligently. The question is: what is the injury and what is appropriate compensation? Society's traditional view is that pregnancy and the birth of a baby are blessed events. Society has changed. It recognizes that the event may not be blessed, but may be tragic or at least inconvenient. The law reflects this new realization, but only partially.

Chief Justice Deschenes recognized that Mrs. Cataford suffered loss of enjoyment of life, inconvenience and anxiety due to the pregnancy, the pain and suffering of the pregnancy itself and the second sterilization which was subsequently performed. His Lordship ordered the surgeon to pay $2000 to Mrs. Cataford in compensation.

The cost of raising Marcel was not considered an injury to Mr. and Mrs. Cataford. They would be, the court said, more than compensated by the moral and financial benefits (from social welfare) they would obtain by his presence in their home.

Mr. Cataford also sued, but since he was blessed by the birth of Marcel, he was found to have suffered no injuries except a temporary loss of marital relations.

## The Birth of a Deformed Baby

The question yet to be answered in Canadian law, at least at the time of this writing, is whether cases like that of the Catafords would be treated differently if the child had been born deformed. As in all negligence cases, it will be necessary to prove that the injury—the rearing of a deformed child—was reasonably foreseeable. An unwanted child was reasonably foreseeable in the Cataford case, but there the benefits outweighed the injury, at least according to the judge. In the case of a deformed child, would the costs outweigh the benefits? The special schools, the special equipment, the uninsured medication? What about the heartache, the frustration and the suffering?

The American courts have been divided on this question. In 1967, the New Jersey Supreme Court denied compensation to the parents of a child born deaf and blind. The court said that if the parents had known that the child would be born deformed, they would have terminated the pregnancy by an abortion. The court said that it would not approve of such an alternative which would violate "the preciousness of human life." The central issue is whether life is considered under all circumstances to be a blessing.

A Texas court in 1975 came to a different conclusion. Instead of trying to determine the value of life with a deformed body as opposed to no life at all, the court simply determined the *additional* costs of raising a deformed child. Recent American cases have followed this approach in the case of deformed children whose parents wish they had never been born. The parents wanted the opportunity to have the pregnancies terminated.

It is an open question whether Canadian courts will compensate parents for raising the negligently-born, defective child. There is nothing in law which would prevent this type of decision. If the defect could not have been predicted, the defendant may not be held responsible. If it was foreseeable, the courts may feel compelled to award compensation. The issue goes far beyond the technicalities of the law.

If the mother knows that the unwanted pregnancy is to result in a defective child, should she be under an obligation to seek an abortion? If she does not, how can she later seek compensation for raising a child who was conceived through the defendant's negligence, but whose birth she could have avoided? Should her moral and religious objections to abortion be taken into consideration? If so, would, the anti-abortion mother win the money necessary to raise the defective child, whereas the pro-abortion woman would be compensated only for the unwanted conception and abortion? If she is against abortion, should she be required to put the defective baby up for adoption?

What would be the effect of such lawsuits on the psychological state of the child? Should this be taken into consideration by Canadian courts? The questions are presently mere speculation.

## Rape

A wrongful birth case brought against a rapist by the victim is in a stronger position than that of the negligently caused birth. In the negligent birth it may be difficult to prove that the child was reasonably foreseeable. In the case of a rape, a birth, while not always occurring, is certainly a reasonable possibility. The rapist is not only responsible because of his rape; because he is the father, he is definitely responsible for all costs including maintenance of the child until the age of majority. It is irrelevant whether the child is deformed or normal. Both the mother and the child have a claim for the child's support and for the costs of the pregnancy. The mother would also have a claim for her own suffering because of the violent assault on her.

A particularly interesting question is whether the victim's husband has a claim. He has no obligation to support the child. Traditionally, however, the old English Common Law gave him the right to sue the person who interfered with his exclusive right to his wife's sexual services. Some provinces still permit this legal action for what is called "criminal conversation." Others have abolished it.

In practice, suits of this nature are so rare as to be almost extinct. It is pointless to sue a rapist who is a "guest" in a government prison and therefore incapable of making enough money to satisfy his legal responsibilities. While some rapists may own property from which one could satisfy a claim, the credit rating of most is less worthy.

## A Wrongful Life

If lawsuits brought by parents for wrongful conception, pregnancy and birth are difficult, lawsuits brought by children for wrongful life are mind-boggling. The thought of a child going to court with the argument that he should not have been born and wants to be compensated for being alive has challenged even the most astute legal minds.

The child, through his or her lawyer, is saying that the defendant failed to abide by average, reasonable and prudent standards and, as a reasonably foreseeable result, he was born. He is saying that his birth and his life are injuries.

In the Quebec case of Mrs. Cataford against Dr. Moreau, the child, Marcel, also sued the doctor through his guardian. Chief Justice Duschenes dismissed his claim. It would be impossible to compare the situation of the child after his birth, to the situation in which he would have found himself, if he had not been born.

The American courts had followed the same logic. Lawsuits brought by a child for his or her wrongful life, as distinct from wrongful birth lawsuits brought by parents, would not be allowed. Even in cases where the child was born defective, the American courts were unanimous. It was impossible for judges to conceive of life in any form, no matter how unpleasant, as not being preferable to non-existence.

The problem has been regarded as one to be left up to the legislatures rather than to the courts. Government should look after deformed children, not the people who negligently caused their birth. Britain took this step in 1976 when it passed the Congenital Disabilities Act. This law provides for compensation to children born severely damaged as a result of vaccines administered in national immunization programs.

Even if it is decided that compensation is needed, the courts are not very well designed to deal with the situation. How can a judge determine that if a child could have chosen, he would have chosen not to be born, to being born defective? Or if existence is better than nonexistence? And if compensation is to be awarded to children born deformed, what prevents lawsuits in other unfortunate circumstances?

A child might sue the person who caused him to be born into an unhappy home with a drunken father and a promiscuous mother. Is this life any better or worse than that of a deformed child in a loving, caring home where initially another child was not wanted?

Even if such actions were permitted by children for wrongful life, it would be extremely difficult for a court to place a price tag on the injury of life. The problem is obviously a social, moral and political one. It cannot be solved by the adversary system of court proceedings.

Despite all of these arguments, basic legal principles could be applied to wrongful life were it not for the judges' revulsion of the idea of suing for being alive. In 1980 this revulsion was overcome. On June 11, the California Court of Appeals shocked the medico-legal world with its decision in *Curlender* v. *Bio-Science Laboratories*. The court recognized a legal action for wrongful life.

In this case, the parents of the child in question underwent laboratory tests to determine whether they were carriers of Tay-Sachs disease, a progressively disabling and fatal disorder which could be passed on to their offspring. They were given incorrect information and as a result did nothing to prevent the conception and birth of a child with the disease.

The child suffered from "mental retardation, susceptibility to other diseases, convulsions, sluggishness, apathy, failure to fix objects with her eyes, inability to take an interest in her surroundings, loss of motor reaction, inability to sit up or hold her head up, loss of weight, muscle atrophy, blindness, pseudobulpar palsy, inability to feed orally, decerebrate rigidity and gross physical deformity." The disease is incurable and gives the infant a life expectancy of four years.

The court said that there is a duty owed by medical laboratories to both parents and to their unborn children. That duty is to use ordinary care in the administration of tests to provide information concerning genetic defects in the unborn. The laboratory failed in this duty and was held responsible to the child for her injuries, as well as to the parents for their suffering. What effect this case will have on future American—and Canadian—lawsuits for wrongful life remains to be seen.

## The Answers

Like answers to all legal problems, answers to these problems rarely take the form of a simple rule binding on all people, at all times, and under all circumstances. The law examines the relations between people, their rights and their duties. Individual situations can affect the legal outcome. In any event, with so few cases of wrongful birth and wrongful life to guide us as precedents, the answers will be speculative, with law professors on both sides of every argument.

The application of the law as it has developed so far makes it possible for the physician to be held responsible for negligently performing a sterilization, or an abortion which fails to terminate a pregnancy and results in the birth of a child. The physician can be responsible for the wrongful birth due to negligent advice regarding fertility or the possibility of a deformed child. Similarly, a pharmacist can be held responsible for negligently dispensing drugs, and the drug manufacturer for negligently producing a drug or device that causes a wrongful birth. Negligent testing by a laboratory giving misleading advice may have a similar result.

While responsibility may be fixed upon these potential wrongdoers, the extent of the responsibility may be limited. It will include compensation for the unwanted pregnancy and delivery, but not for the raising of a healthy but unwanted and negligently deformed child whose handicap was reasonably foreseeable. At present, this is uncertain in Canada. It is unlikely to include responsibility to the child for wrongful life, though California's influence could be felt north of the American border.

## The Ultimate Question

If law is a true reflection of society, one is forced to conclude that society has gone through a radical revolution within the last 20 years. Despite the fact that for millions of people, at least in the western world, living standards have never been higher, there is growing realization that life may not be a gift. Millions support the greater availability of abortions and back their arguments with the same moral fervor as those opposing abortion. There is a growing trend to allow "death with dignity" for terminally ill patients rather than to preserve life at all costs. It is logical, therefore, that society and the law have concluded that pregnancy, birth and life may be viewed as injuries rather than gifts. It thus stands to reason that death may not always be an injury. It may be considered a gift.

# 6 The Legal Cost of Sex

## A Price Tag on Sex

Everything has its price—including sex. What is the price tag on two months of sex lost from injuries in a car accident? Or the value of a lifetime of sex lost due to medical malpractice? A price tag must also be assigned to lost or injured sexual organs. It is a difficult task. The monetary value of a penis, a vagina, a vulva or one or two testicles is hard to determine. Likewise, sexual functions have their value. A perplexing challenge lies in the determination of the value of ejaculation, erection, fertility and orgasm. Judges and juries have been asked to face this challenge.

There are two situations in which the courts will be asked to put a price tag on the value of sex, or on the value of sexual organs. The first relates to a person who has been injured due to the fault of another. The injury has either made it impossible to have sexual relations or possible to have sexual relations only with a great deal of pain or difficulty. The injury may not have interfered with the sexual act, but did make it impossible to have children. The injured party takes legal action and asks the court for compensation. The judge, or sometimes a judge and jury, cannot give the person back what has been lost, but can force the wrongdoer to pay a certain amount of money sufficient to compensate the injured person. The questions is: how much?

The second situation involving lost sex concerns a married couple.

The wife has been injured. She is no longer able to provide for her husband's sexual needs. While she may have a claim against the wrongdoer for her injuries, her husband also has suffered a loss. He may also sue the wrongdoer. The question arises: How much is his loss worth?

## How the Courts Price Injuries

Over the years courts in Canada, Britain, the United States and elsewhere have developed certain basic principles for awarding money damages to compensate for injuries wrongfully caused by others. These injuries are not restricted to sex, but range from lost legs, mangled intestines, paraplegia to brain damage—the list of horrors parading through Canadian courts is unending. The tragedies inflicted by Canadians against other Canadians confront judges and juries from coast to coast every day. In each of these cases, a price tag must be assigned to the tragedy. The purpose of this price tag is to force the wrongdoer to pay this amount to the injured party. The theory is, as Lord Blackburn said in England in 1880, to put the injured party in the same position as he or she would have been if no injury had been suffered.

In setting the amount of an award to be given to a victim for his or her injuries, the law determines what type of award (or what the law calls "damages") is to be given. There are three types. The first is called "nominal." It is a very small amount, awarded when the person suing has not suffered any substantial loss or injury, but whose legal rights have technically been violated. A surgeon who amputated a man's hand against his wishes, even though the amputation was necessary, was ordered to pay nominal damages of $50. That was in 1935. Now the courts regard this type of malpractice as requiring more than nominal damages and would probably want to punish the doctor. In doing so, they would order him to pay what are known as "punitive" damages. This amount is ordered either on its own or in addition to other damages. It is awarded not to compensate the victim, even though he gets the money, but to punish the wrongdoer. It is not enough for the act which caused the injury to have been wrong, such as negligent driving, or the failure to clear ice from one's steps. It will only be awarded when the conduct of the wrongdoer is deemed aggravated, willful or wanton. Performing an unnecessary hysterectomy on a young, married woman during a routine appendectomy without her permission would likely justify punitive damages.

The third category of award is "compensatory" damage, or what some courts have called "actual" damage. While nominal and punitive damages are relatively infrequent, compensatory damages make up the vast bulk of court awards. These monetary sums are designed to compensate, or to repay the victim in dollars for his injury or loss.

Some compensatory damages are not too difficult to calculate. These are the "special damages" or "specials." These include actual expenses, which the victim has been forced to pay, such as hospital, medical and drug bills over and above anything paid for by provincial health insurance programs. Lost wages, the repair of an automobile or the repair of teeth smashed by an assailant can be calculated exactly. There may be arguments over whether a particular bill has been inflated, or whether the repairs were really necessary, or whether the damage was really caused by the defendant at all. These can be settled, however, usually with accuracy and often to the exact cent.

## Pricing the Nonreplaceable

The real stickler is how to determine general compensatory damages. This is the award given to compensate the victim for those injuries which do not ordinarily have a monetary value. The court cannot replace the hand that no longer works because of someone's negligence, the eye that cannot see, the shortened life, the scars, the loss of sexual ability, the pain, the suffering or the torment. While the court cannot actually put the injured party back in the position he was in before the injury, the court can order the wrongdoer to pay the victim money. There is no magic formula used to determine this amount. It is arrived at simply by guesswork. The judges and juries are guided by what other judges have guessed at in similar cases. If they go too far off the mark and one or both of the parties appeal, the appeal court will change the order to fall in line with previous guesses.

How else can one set a value on the loss of those things which have no price and which cannot be replaced? It may be very easy for a faceless insurance company in Toronto to say that the loss of a hand in Corner Brook or Kelowna is worth $5000 regardless of who lost the hand. Fortunately, the law is usually more humane than insurance companies. The loss of a hand to a 25-year-old machinist supporting a wife and three children is worth considerably more than the loss of the hand of a retired, widowed radio announcer. While one may agree that the 25-year-old had suffered more monetarily, who knows who has suffered the most emotionally?

# The Price of Sexual Injuries

The same difficulties are compounded when applied to sexual injuries. The loss of a hand or a leg can affect income. A scar on the face of a model can result in unemployment. If, however, an injury results in sexual relations with great pain, is the value of that injury greater if the victim is a married man or woman accustomed to regular intercourse than if the victim is an elderly, and largely celibate bachelor? If a doctor negligently sterilizes a nun not far from menopause, is that a cheaper wrongful act than sterilizing a young married woman hoping for more children? How does the judge or the jury step into the shoes of the victim to determine the value of the hurt?

The law talks about awarding reasonable damages, of compensating but not rewarding. Being a victim is not supposed to produce a windfall. No specific rules, however, are given. Perhaps none can be. So much depends on how the judge or jury reacted to the victim. Did the victim arouse sympathy? Was he a "deserving" injured man, or will an award be given on the basis of his bare legal rights alone?

One wonders how the personal background of judges and jurors affects the amount of the general damages awarded. What impact will their sense of morality have on the damages awarded? Assume that the victim is a junior executive, with two children, a charming wife, a house in the suburbs, who reads nothing more exciting than *Reader's Digest*. He has been injured by the negligence of another automobile driver and can no longer have sexual intercourse with his wife. His was a model all-Canadian family. However, assume that the victim with the same injuries is a middle-aged, unmarried playboy. He has no intention of getting married. His life, in fact his entire world, revolves around having sex with every woman he can pick up—and with every man. Without his merry-go-round life of sexual adventures, his life is empty. How sympathetic will the court be? Will his award be the same as that given to the junior executive? These questions remain unanswered.

# Canada v. the United States in Damage Awards

Canadian newspapers regularly report court awards for personal injuries in the millions of dollars. As is often the case with the Canadian media, the stories are strictly American in origin. Activities in Canadian courts are often overlooked. In reading about the huge damage awards in the United States, it is important to realize that there are major differences between the Canadian and American systems which may account for this disparity.

The first major distinction is that most American court awards involving personal injuries are set by juries. In Canada, a high proportion of such cases are tried by a judge alone. Jury trials are either unavailable due to provincial court practice or because the plaintiff requests that a judge alone hear his case.

The second major distinction between the two countries is in the size of the awards. Court awards in excess of $1 million are far more frequent in the United States for loss of enjoyment of life, pain and suffering, out-of-pocket expenses, lost wages and mental anguish, as well as for hospital and medical costs. Even the most serious injuries in Canada would bring in only a few hundred thousand dollars. Canadians of the "me too" school of thinking, who take their cue from "south of the border," may be outraged at this discrepancy. They forget that Americans have nothing comparable to the Canadian universal hospital insurance and medicare programs. These programs cover the ever-increasing costs of present and future hospitalizations and doctors' bills, which make up a large part of the million dollar awards.

Despite the Canadian medical programs, a Canadian body may seem to be worth far less than that of an American. The loss of an eye, a hand, a functioning bladder or a uterus may appear to be worth far more in Atlanta than in Lethbridge. Americans place a higher money value on personal injuries than do Canadians. The high cost of their health care may be largely to blame, but any precise explanation of the difference is mere speculation. Americans, it is said, see everything in terms of money and try to balance the injury with a pot of gold which may provide the enjoyment the victim has lost. Canadians and their legal system, lacking the political philosophy of the United States, are not concerned with "life, liberty and the pursuit of happiness." The status quo of the realities of life is accepted. Misfortunes occur in life as part of living. They cannot be avoided and cannot be corrected, neither by the courts, by the government nor by dollar bills. The award is meant to compensate the injured person, not to create enormous profits for him. The courts recognize that complete compensation is never possible and that the vengeance of a massive award could cause injustice to the wrongdoer far beyond what he deserves. There is also the recognition that large awards may never be collected because the wrongdoer simply does not have that amount of money.

There are certain factors which can reduce the amount of money awarded to a victim for personal injuries—or even cut him out entirely. A court may find that the victim was partially to blame for his own injuries and will reduce his award accordingly. He may be found entirely responsible and will receive no compensation at all.

## Paying the Price

The defendant cannot be held responsible for damages which he could not have reasonably foreseen. Nor will he be responsible for injuries which may or may not occur in the future. These are too uncertain. Applying these principles to sexual injuries, it is apparent that a claim for sexual loss is difficult to prove. In fact, in 1960 the flamboyant American trial attorney Melvin Belli said that claims for the actual loss of reproductive organs were infrequent. The situation has not changed in the last 20 years. Neither Canadians nor Americans sue very often *solely* because they have lost the use of their sexual facilities. What usually happens is that sexual functions are lost along with more extensive and debilitating injuries. An overall award of general damages is then given for pain, suffering and loss of enjoyment of life. The award is not itemized for individual injuries. A number of Canadian cases prove this point.

The trial division of the Nova Scotia Supreme Court had this problem in the case of *Spicer* v. *Chappell* in 1979. As the result of a motor vehicle accident, a woman required five operations. She was left with ugly scars on her legs, which caused her much embarrassment, a detrimental change in her personality, her knees were no longer at the same level and she suffered back and leg pains. In addition she had to be sterilized. In assessing the nonpecuniary damages, the various injuries were not given a value. The judge simply set a total award of $30,000.

Overall awards compensating victims for injury to sexual organs also do not distinguish or separate out the injuries to organs with other functions. The injury may affect not only sexual performance but urinary function, as well. No attempt is made to put a price on each of these losses. An overall award covers everything.

On October 3, 1977 the Ontario Court of Appeal was faced with a woman who was injured and as a result required a hysterectomy and lost a potential child. The sum awarded to her was $25,000.

In British Columbia in 1976, a Vancouver court, in the case of *Gilbert* v. *Campbell*, set damages for an infant who, during circumcision, lost part of his penis. The court would not take into account the possibility that the child might suffer embarrassment in the future. This was considered to be too speculative. The award was $750.

Over 26 years before, a Manitoba court, in the case of *Gray* v. *LaFleche*, dealt with a very similar injury. The negligent circumcision resulted in almost the total removal of the glans penis, that part of the penis which extends beyond the foreskin. Medical experts predicted that the child would be able to have sex and to reproduce, though sensation would be reduced to some extent. Further surgery, however, would be necessary to remove the scar tissue. Of major concern was the possible psychological effect of a deformed penis on an otherwise normal, healthy child. It could also diminish his chances of marriage. These latter concerns were mere possibilities, not probabilities. The doctor's lawyer argued that because they were mere speculation, the court should not take them into consideration. The court disagreed. The other argument for the defense was that the diminution of marriage possibilities was not an injury and should not be compensated. The court disagreed and awarded the child $10,000.

One may ask whether the value of a penis has decreased between the 1950 Manitoba case and the 1976 British Columbia case. Or is this particular organ of greater value in Manitoba than it is on the coast? Again there are no answers. So much depends on how extensive the injury was and how moved the judge was by the testimony of the medical experts as to its severity.

The issue of decreased marriage prospects was not a new one. It had been accepted as an injury worthy of compensation back in 1909 by the Ontario Court of Appeal in *Morin* v. *Ottawa Electric Railway Company.* In that case a 21-year-old woman was run over by one of the defendant company's cars. She lost her leg and the control of a hand and an arm. This was particularly serious since she was a stenographer. In addition to the pain and suffering and the loss of her vocation, the court said that in setting the award the jury was entitled to take into consideration the effect of the accident upon her marriage prospects. The total award was $5,500.

The most difficult problem in compensating sexual injuries arises in cases concerning a husband who has lost the sexual enjoyment of his wife due to injuries which she has suffered. How much is this loss worth? How much should the person who wrongfully injured the wife have to pay for interfering with the husband's right to sexual relations with her?

In 1978, Chief Justice Deschenes of the Quebec Superior Court was forced to decide that question. In the case of *Cataford* v. *Moreau,* which was discussed in Chapter Four, Monsieur Cataford had lost approximately two months of benefits of his wife's consortium, which in this case was mainly sex. His Lordship compensated Monsieur Cataford by awarding him $400.

An Alberta court in the same year placed the loss of consortium of a wife at $1,000 in *Jagorinec* v. *Ryan*. The New Brunswick Court of Queen's Bench gave a husband the same amount in *Tracy* v. *Morrison*. In that case, however, the wife was in hospital for 23 days and unwell for over a year. The year before, a Manitoba court in *Farmer* v. *Richard* lumped all aspects of consortium together. Loss of companionship, love, affection, comfort, mental services and sexual intercourse for 18 months was valued at $3,500.

## How the Courts Define Consortium

It should be noted that there is a great wrangle in the courts over whether consortium means the whole marital relationship or simply sex. The Ontario courts say that if the husband has lost the totality of his wife's company and services, he can sue. If he has simply lost sexual relations, the judges, at least in Ontario, will not compensate him. The principle behind this position is that the law should protect the entire marital relationship, not just one aspect of it. In Ontario the conclusion is clear: a husband cannot sue for impairment or diminution of marital relations, sexual powers, sexual pleasure or activities.

A related issue is the temporary loss or diminished enjoyment of marital relations. Can a person sue for the partial or temporary loss of consortium? In some provinces, notably in British Columbia, Alberta, Saskatchewan and Quebec the courts have said "yes." However, courts in Manitoba and Ontario have said "no." In these provinces, one must sue on an "all or nothing" basis where consortium is concerned.

Until fairly recently, all cases for loss of consortium (which included sex) were brought by husbands who had lost the pleasure of their wives' company and service. Service is to be defined in the broadest way possible. Under English Common Law, the husband had a right to his wife's company and service. He could sue if that right had been interfered with by the wrongdoer injuring the wife. On the wife's part, it was clearly recognized by the House of Lords as late as 1952 that the wife had no such right. One could say that anything of that variety, which she enjoyed, amounted to a privilege.

The reason for this inequity was that in the Middle Ages a woman was under the protection and support of her father until marriage and her husband after marriage. Women as the weaker sex required protection in this rather brutal age and the law gave it to them. The woman was also part and parcel of the man's estate from which he received numerous services. Any attack on the wife was in effect an attack on the man and his estate, his goods, his chattels. An attack on the man, however, did not interfere with any right the woman had, unless the man could no longer provide her with support and protection.

While today's emancipated woman may bristle at the thought of these inequities, the law did reflect the social structure of the times and the strictly defined sexual roles. It is only within very recent times that attitudes among some people have begun to change. If the current trend continues, the law, as a reflection of society, will eventually follow suit. Signs of change are already noticeable. The question is whether the wife should also be allowed to sue for the loss of her husband's consortium, or whether the husband should lose his long-established legal right to sue for the loss of his wife's consortium. British Columbia and Ontario have abolished the right to sue for consortium, though Ontario has allowed a spouse to sue for certain injuries resulting from injury to his or her spouse. Alberta has extended the right to wives.

In addition to suits for the loss of consortium due to the negligence of a third party, the Old English Common Law recognized the wrongful act of criminal conversation. This was actually neither "criminal" nor "conversation," though some of the latter may have been involved. It was defined as one man having sex with another man's wife. The cuckolded husband was permitted to sue his wife's adulterer for criminal conversation and claim damages to compensate him for his loss of honor and for the loss of his monopoly over his wife's services. When a husband sued for loss of consortium, he was complaining about someone's unintentional but negligent act, which interfered with his right to consortium, because of the wife's injuries. In criminal conversation, he was complaining about the intentional act of his wife's lover in luring his wife away from him.

The right to sue for criminal conversation was abolished in England in 1857. Canada, apart from Quebec, having received its law from England, was determined to hang on to it. The Atlantic provinces, Manitoba and Saskatchewan still have it. It was abolished in Ontario in 1978. As with a suit for loss of consortium, only a husband can sue for criminal conversation, except in the liberated province of Alberta where wives have been given the right.

Even where it is still possible to sue for criminal conversation, actions have been infrequent. Either Canadian husbands have tough skins and are not about to sue their wives' lovers or they simply sue for divorce. The real answer probably lies in the fact that Canadian judges think that the feelings of a cuckolded husband are not worth much. It is not worth suing.

## The Problem of Cause and Effect

In any discussion of sexual injuries, a practical problem faces the trial lawyer. It may be possible to prove to a court that the defendant committed a wrongful act against the plaintiff. It may also be possible to prove that the plaintiff has lost certain sexual abilities or advantages following the defendant's action. What cannot always be proven is that the injury was the reasonably foreseeable result of the defendant's action. It may be too remote.

In the 1976 British Columbia case of *Antell* v. *Simons,* a woman was injured in a car accident due to the negligence of the defendant. She was not seriously hurt but suffered an emotional reaction which prevented her from having sexual intercourse with her husband. Within a year, the husband left her and a divorce followed. The wife had no right to sue for loss of consortium, but she did claim that the defendant's negligent driving had resulted in the destruction of her marriage. Her claim was rejected. The negligent driver could not reasonably have foreseen that his negligent driving would cause a marriage break up and therefore he was not responsible for it.

## How to Pay the Price

Placing a money value on sex will never be an easy task. Compensating injuries will never be easy. Since money is the only means of compensation available, it will never be totally satisfactory. As inflation continues, the cost of sexual and other injuries will increase. As long as human beings are to decide the fates of other human beings, the amounts awarded will vary from case to case. The alternative of a standard list of damage awards would provide certainty, but would remove humanity from the decision-making process in the courts. As in all of society's decisions, this could be good or bad, depending on the case. There is no answer.

# 7 V.D.—
# The Wages of Sin

Everyone blames it on someone else. The English called it the French disease. The French called it the Spanish disease; the Japanese, the Chinese disease; and the Chinese, the Canton disease. Today, venereal disease has, according to Health and Welfare Canada, reached epidemic proportions. Although it cuts across all social and economic classes, we still try to lay the blame on others: on truckers, bikers, Indians, homosexuals, prostitutes and on people on welfare—but never on the boy or girl next door. The disease is still cloaked in mystery.

Many think that society has become too liberated. Young ladies from good families live openly with their boyfriends and tell all the world. Many women have their babies out of wedlock, keep them and tell everyone. Young men announce to their families, friends and the news media that they are having sex with other young men. With all of this openness, honesty and supposed throwing off of hypocricy, why are people so ashamed to tell their friends that they have V.D.?

Venereal disease was never exclusive to one class. The poor, soldiers, sailors and prostitutes have had it, but so have the mighty and the famous. It is suspected that the list of victims includes Charles VIII and Francis I of France, Pope Alexander Borgia, the artists Benvenuto Cellini and Toulouse-Lautrec, the authors Heinrich Heine and Guy de Maupassant, and also Ivan the Terrible, Henry VIII, George III and Scott Joplin.

There are several theories as to how it got into Europe (since it obviously has to be blamed on someone else). One is that either the sailors with Columbus picked it up in the West Indies or that the natives brought by Columbus to Spain introduced it and gave it to the "civilized" world. Another theory is that Portuguese sailors brought it back from Africa in 1442. In any case, it appeared in Europe at some point in the 15th century and soon spread to India, China, Japan and the rest of the world.

Despite all the jokes about "innocently" contracted venereal disease, for all practical purposes, it can only be contracted by sexual intercourse or transmitted directly from a mother to a baby prior to or during birth. While it is possible to become infected by kissing or breastfeeding, these means are most uncommon, at least in Canada. Given the right conditions, it is even possible to catch it from a toilet seat, but the chances are negligible.

## What is V.D.?

When we talk of venereal or sexually transmitted disease, we are talking in fact about a type of disease, not a particular disease. There are five venereal diseases that are recognized by law in most Canadian provinces, even though there are others. These five are syphilis, gonorrhea, chancroid, granuloma inguinale and lymphogranuloma venereum. New Brunswick recognizes only the first three by name, and all others that are diagnosed simply as venereal disease by a medical practitioner. Newfoundland recognizes only the first four. In fact, gonorrhea and syphilis are the two most prevalent.

Gonorrhea is the more "popular." According to Health and Welfare Canada, it is probably the most common communicable disease in the country. It attacks males two to five days after infection, though in rare cases the symptoms will not appear for six weeks. Usually there is sudden, frequent and painful urination. There is often a thick, creamy discharge, whitish-yellow in color though this may be painless. The opening of the penis becomes red and swollen. Symptoms may also appear in the rectal area and bacteria may be found in the stools, particularly from infection due to passive homosexual activity. The disease may appear in the throat of men and women as a result of oral-genital contact. About 15 to 20 percent of men and up to 80 percent of women, however, have no symptoms at all. In women the disease attacks the cervix, the uterus, the fallopian tubes and the rectum. Various complications can result, including arthritis and on rare occasions, meningitis.

A most tragic result of gonorrhea is the infection of the newborn baby as it is leaving the mother and passing through her infected cervix. It can cause severe eye damage and even blindness. Fortunately, a preventive measure can be taken by placing one drop of one percent silver nitrate solution in each of the baby's eyes, a practice which has become routine in hospitals.

Because so many V.D.-infected people have no symptoms, but are carriers and infect others, it is common practice to treat anyone who has been exposed to someone who has gonorrhea. While the treatment is not complicated, follow-up care is required to make certain that the patient is cured.

Syphilis, on the other hand, spreads to the entire body within a few hours of infection. The patient will not be aware of it for three to four weeks, at which point a painless chancre may form on the cervix or in the vagina (where it will go unnoticed), or on or around the genital organs. It could also appear around the anus of the passive male homosexual or the woman who has been sodomized, or in the throat or mouth of those infected by oral contact. Without treatment, the chancre will disappear in a few weeks. The patient, however, has just been through the primary stage.

The patient will then enter the secondary stage and two to six weeks later, the latent stage. He or she may fluctuate back and forth between the secondary and latent stages for about a year. There may be a skin rash, a mild fever or a feeling of discomfort. There is little to alarm the patient. In the primary and secondary stages, however, the disease is infectious. The early latent stage is sometimes infectious, sometimes not.

The latent stage may be with the patient for the rest of his or her life without any effect. He or she may die from other causes. The disease may disappear by itself or, as in about one-third of all untreated cases, it will enter the tertiary stage. It is this stage which is so terrible.

It can enter this stage from three to even 40 years following the intercourse which initially infected the patient. The two most serious results are cardiovascular syphilis and neurosyphilis. The first so severely damages the heart that death by heart failure may result.

Neurosyphilis frequently results in headaches, insomnia, memory defects, loss of ability to concentrate, irritability, temper tantrums, slurred speech, delusions of grandeur, personality tremors, and eventually, what has been called general paralysis of the insane. The patient becomes a helpless maniac.

Up to the end of the 19th century, venereal disease was virtually incurable. Penicillin came on the scene in the 20th century and has been heralded as the magic cure-all. To a large extent, if administered properly, it is. In the last few years, however, strains of V.D. have been discovered that are resistant to penicillin and other antibiotics. The consequences could be frightening.

## V.D. and the Criminal Law

Governments throughout the world have attempted to control V.D. through law because it is so highly contagious and serious if left untreated. Given the nature of the illness and the means by which it is contracted, these attempts have been remarkably unsuccessful. Every province and territory has special legislation regarding venereal disease quite apart from legislation dealing with other communicable diseases, such as diphtheria and tuberculosis. These statutes and regulations impose basic duties on both patients and physicians. In fact, many of them interfere with basic civil rights more than almost any other law on the books. One wonders how much of this is necessary and what effect they have on the control of the disease.

The first duty, which is imposed on citizens is imposed not as a public health matter, but as a criminal matter. The Parliament of Canada has placed in the Criminal Code the following as subsection (1) of section 253. "Everyone who, having venereal disease in a communicable form, communicates it to another person is guilty of an offence punishable on summary conviction." Statistics Canada has no record of anyone ever having been convicted under this section. This is not surprising. Parliament has tried to tell Canadians when they can and cannot have sex. One wonders whether the politicians were so naive to believe that anyone infected with V.D. and about to have sexual intercourse would be thinking of the House of Commons.

Working on the assumption that such a prohibition would be effective, Parliament felt sympathy for the person who "innocently" gave V.D. to someone or as the law so gently puts it "communicated" it. Thus subsection (2) was passed in case a person cither thought he did not have V.D., or thought that it was not contagious. It reads: "No person shall be convicted of an offence under this section where he proves that he had reasonable grounds to believe and did believe that he did not have venereal disease in a communicable form at the time the offence is alleged to have been committed." It is not enough to have such a belief; one must have reasonable grounds for the belief. One wonders what these might be.

Because of the danger of false accusations, no one is convicted by the evidence of only one witness. More than one is required. The Code states: "No person shall be convicted of an offence under this section upon the evidence of only one witness, unless the evidence of that witness is corroborated in a material particular by evidence that implicates the accused." Given the intimacy of the sexual act and the delicacy of the situation, such evidence would be at least difficult, if not impossible, to find. With all these loopholes to contend with, prosecutors face monumental tasks. So monumental, no doubt, that Crown prosecutors often choose easier crimes to prosecute.

As a footnote, it is interesting to note that one can only be convicted if the disease is syphilis, gonorrhea or soft chancre (chancroid). If a person suffers from any other type of V.D., even if he or she knowingly gives it to someone else, it is no crime. At one time the criminal law was much harsher. It was an offense to communicate a disease by what was called "culpable negligence." In 1926, the Saskatchewan Court of Appeal sentenced a Mr. Leaf to 12 months of hard labor in the Regina Gaol for giving V.D. to a woman who died as a result.

So much for federal control of what goes on in the bedrooms of the nation. V.D. is a provincial matter and that is where one must look for the bulk of the law.

## V.D. and the Provinces

A number of provinces have tried to attack the problem by placing the initial duty on the patient. British Columbia, Alberta, Saskatchewan, Ontario, New Brunswick, Prince Edward Island and Newfoundland require that every person infected with, or suspecting, V.D. go to a doctor. Taking the principle of the "supremacy of Parliament" at face value, the legislators of Prince Edward Island, Ontario and British Columbia have followed their Ottawa cousins. They have all passed legislation stating, "Every person shall conduct himself in such a manner as not to expose other persons to the danger of infection." In other words: no sex!

## Compulsory Reporting

The second duty imposed by law is on the doctor. V.D., like many other communicable diseases is, in most places in Canada, considered to be a notifiable disease. This means that any physician who becomes aware that someone is suffering from the disease has a legal obligation to notify a public health official, usually the local medical officer of health.

The controversial problem concerns what the doctor has to report. In Quebec, the patient is to be designated by a number, age, sex and municipality of residency. No name is used *unless* the patient refuses to take treatment. In British Columbia the law specifically requires the name to be reported. Legislation elsewhere in Canada requires physicians to report cases of V.D. they encounter. It is not clear whether the patients have to be named.

The effect of laws requiring doctors to report the names of V.D. patients is that it breaks the traditional bond of secrecy between doctor and patient. Because doctors are unwilling to do this, only about 25 percent of all V.D. cases in Canada are reported. Doctors have no such reluctance about reporting other communicable diseases. This unwillingness is probably due to V.D. not being seen as a major public health hazard as is diphtheria. It is also due to the patients' embarrassment of having V.D., since it invites wagging fingers and loose tongues. The community really does not believe that clerks in public health offices will keep their mouths shut, no matter how principled they may be. The law is no match for society's feelings.

If the law just required reporting the number of cases seen by a doctor, social concern might not be as strong. The reporting of the names of V.D. patients, however, sets in motion the "contact tracing system." This system is based on the theory that the sexual partner or partners of the infected person may also have V.D. If he or she divulges the name or names, public officials can track them down, treat them and find out who were their contacts.

It is argued by many that the system is a disaster. Manitoba regulations require the patient to divulge "the source of infection." The critics ask, "How many people are going to tell a public health official who they have slept with?" How often will the truthful answer be, "Some girl I met on the bus from Saskatoon?" How often will the patient be unwilling to tell, truthfully cannot remember or simply does not know? The last is particularly true in the homosexual community where sexual contacts may be very fleeting, very frequent and, according to public health studies, very contagious.

Even if patients did divulge willingly the names (and there are often many) of their contacts, by the time the disease is apparent, treatment is sought and the contact tracing begun, weeks have passed. The contact has often had many other contacts, each of whom has had contacts. The pyramid of those infected has grown quickly and passed through many levels since the initial report, even though not all the contacts may have contracted the disease. Moreover, not all the contacts may have had further sexual relations or have had relations with the same frequency. It is also argued that the system breaks down because, in our very mobile society, many of the contacts cannot be traced.

If one could be immunized against V.D., there might be some hope of controlling it. In the present state, once a patient is treated, he or she can go out the door and become infected again. Some V.D. clinics have found that the patients waiting for their treatment got to know each other—so well that they undid what the clinic had just done. Having separate homes or rooms for men and women did not completely remove all opportunity for sexual introductions.

Many believe that the reporting laws are totally unworkable and argue that the laws should be abolished. The laws are often ignored by doctors with the grateful consent of their patients. The laws are seen as an affront to the doctor's oath of secrecy. It is asked whether the reporting requirements provide sufficient information to protect the public's health. In all likelihood, there are not, nor ever will be, enough public health officials to follow through effectively.

## Compulsory Treatment

A more important aspect of venereal disease legislation is that of compulsory treatment. One of our very basic civil rights is the right to remain untouched by others. For this reason, Canadians who are mentally capable may refuse to take treatment, even though the failure to take treatment may result in their death. There are, however, several rights which conflict with the right to remain untouched, the first being that police officers and penal officials may use reasonable physical force in carrying out their duties. The second is that a person may use reasonable physical force to protect himself, his family or his property. Thirdly, under provincial legislation, in certain more dangerous cases involving mental illness, a person may be taken, confined and treated by force. The fourth concerns the case of a communicable disease which is a danger to the public at large. V.D. falls into this category.

Some question whether V.D. should be considered in a way similar to other communicable diseases. It is said that the others are truly public health hazards, since anyone can get them by innocently passing by, or coming into minimal personal contact with, the carrier of the disease. V.D. is not caught so casually. The contact must be of a most intimate and personal nature, which those engaging in it have the freedom to undertake. One of the risks of a union between persons not well-known to one another is venereal disease. The risk of V.D. is inherent. The parties can either refrain from sex or take precautions, such as using condoms, to minimize the risks. Persons contracting other communicable diseases may have no such choice. They are not engaging in activities which carry a risk of these diseases. Therefore, they are truly a public health hazard and the law steps in to force treatment on those who refuse it. V.D., it can be argued, is not contracted in this way and is only a hazard to those engaging in sexual activities with people they do not know well enough to be sure of the risks involved. This is not really a hazard to the public. The law should not force those who refuse treatment to have it simply to protect those who should protect themselves. So goes the argument. It has not won the day. The law does provide for the compulsory treatment of V.D.

Every province and territory has legislation to force people to be examined for V.D. The power of public health officials to compel a person to be examined for V.D. is enormous. The procedure removes rights that even those charged with serious criminal offences are guaranteed. In a criminal trial the onus is on the Crown prosecutor to prove the accusation, not simply to the satisfaction of the judge and jury, but beyond a reasonable doubt.

In Newfoundland, for example, when a medical health officer has reasonable grounds for believing that any person is or may be infected with venereal disease, or has been exposed to infection, he may order that person to be examined and to produce a certificate detailing the results. The only possible appeal would be to convince a court that the officer did not have the authority to issue the order, since he did not have "reasonable grounds for believing." This would be a difficult if not a hopeless task. Failure to comply with such an order "without reasonable excuse" may result in a fine of up to $500 or imprisonment not exceeding six months.

This type of legislation is not unusual. In Saskatchewan, the minister of health or medical health officer may order anyone to be examined. The person may also be detained until the results are known. In that province, the person making the order does not even need to have "reasonable grounds" for believing that infection is present. It is enough if they have "reason to believe" that the person is infected; a subtle, but important difference.

In Saskatchewan as in many other provinces, if the person who is ordered to be examined refuses, the minister or the medical health officer may apply to a magistrate for an order to have the person appear before the court. The onus is not on the minister or on the medical health officer to show why they need the person examined, the way it would be on the prosecution to prove its case. The onus is on the suspect to show why the examination should not take place.

Alberta is more traditional in its view of justice. There, the magistrate only issues a warrant for detention and examination if a case "has been made out." If the examination proves that the individual has V.D., the law comes down with a vengeance.

In Ontario, when a provincial judge finds that any person "(a) is infected with a venereal disease and is unwilling or unable to conduct himself in such a manner as not to expose other persons to the danger of infection; or (b) is infected with a venereal disease and refuses or neglects to take or continue treatment..." the judge shall order that such a person be admitted to, and detained in, a place of detention for not in excess of one year, as he may consider necessary. In most criminal offenses the judge has a choice as to whether or not to send the accused to jail, but not if he has V.D. In this case, he must be confined for treatment.

Most provinces have similar legislation but it is rarely enforced. An exception is Nova Scotia where, until a few years ago, there were regulations permitting the enforced detention and treatment of those infected with V.D. There was such turmoil over one particular victim of public health zeal, that the regulations were abolished. The new regulations do not appear to have affected the sexual activity of Nova Scotians—or the consequences.

If the missionary fervor of the law seems heavy-handed when reaching out to the public, it is meek in comparison to its zeal towards those employed to enforce it. In Ontario, when a medical officer of health believes that any person in custody "has been or may be infected or has been exposed to infection with venereal disease," he may have that person examined. This applies to anybody under arrest or in custody, including those who have not been convicted of any offense. The medical officer's belief may be totally unfounded. What is even more serious is the officer may direct that the person remain in custody until the results of the examination are known. This results in the incarceration of someone who may be totally innocent of any crime and may not have V.D., simply because some medical officer of health believes that the prisoner may be paying "the wages of sin."

If the prisoner is found to be infected, continued incarceration may be ordered with treatment, regardless of the prisoner's consent. This detention and compulsory treatment can continue until the prisoner is cured or "until he has received a degree of treatment" considered adequate by the attending physician and the Minister (of Health)." Since reinfection can take place within hours of release by merely having sex with someone who is infected, one questions the value of a law which allows for the removal of basic liberty to carry out a health procedure of questionable value. Even more frightening is the possibility of continued reinfection from homosexual activity while in custody. This has been considered by the Ontario legislature and the law allows for the prisoner's isolation. Similar legislation exists in most provinces.

## Miscellaneous Controls

Legislatures throughout the world have attempted to control the spread of V.D. by imposing numerous restrictions. Given the fact that the disease keeps spreading among millions of people, they do not appear to have been very effective. Unlike in Canada, most American states require a medical certificate confirming the absence of V.D. before a marriage license is issued. Many other countries, from Tunisia to Romania, have similar laws. They all rely on one assumption—that sexual relations take place only inside of marriage. By preventing the marriage, one wonders how many innocent young men or women are being protected from their infected fiancés.

Another assumption, acted on in Saskatchewan, is that venereal disease is spread by people who meet at certain establishments. If the establishments are closed, they will not meet. No sex; no V.D.—at least from that source. Thus the Saskatchewan minister of public health, or a medical health officer with the minister's approval, may order the closure of any dance hall, restaurant, hotel, lodging house or other premises of a public nature, if he is satisfied that "persons are contracting venereal disease from persons met" in these places and that they are "accordingly a menace to the health of the community." These powers, however, are not to be exercised until the person in charge has been notified of the menace and, within a period of time specified in the notice, has failed "to take action to prevent the further spread of venereal disease, through persons met or sexually exposed on the premises." One wonders what action is supposed to be taken. The law is silent. One's imagination runs wild.

This action of closing down someone's business is based solely on the minister's opinion. There is no appeal to the courts. The only appeal is to the minister himself, and his decision is final.

Is the closure of private business without any of the ordinary civil rights worth the price of V.D.? If it is, does it really reduce the spread of the disease? If the premises are closed, will infected persons fail to meet other persons? Will sexual activity decrease and the red lights of Regina be dimmed forever?

The only truly effective legislation preventing the transmission of V.D. to the innocent is that involving newborns. By practice or by regulations, silver nitrate is placed in the eyes of newborns to prevent blindness in case the mothers had been infected with gonorrhea. Legislation such as this is effective because it is applied to a situation wholly within the control of the hospital. It does not attempt to control that which is uncontrollable (at least by government), namely sex.

## Advertising Controls

Many quack treatments were being sold for venereal disease during the 19th century and even well into the 20th century. Effective treatment for it is historically quite recent. Even after the discovery of an effective cure, many people either did not know about it or were embarrassed to go to their doctor for it. The fact that the law requires the doctor to report the case to public health officials may also discourage patients from seeking medical attention.

To prevent the travelling medicine men, the quacks and the charlatans from causing harm, the Criminal Code of Canada makes it an offense to knowingly, without lawful justification or excuse, advertise or publish an advertisement of any means, instructions, medicine, drug or article intended or represented as a method for restoring sexual virility or curing venereal diseases or diseases of the genital organs. This prohibition is included in a list of other prohibited acts including the selling, exhibiting or possessing of obscene matter and the exhibiting of a disgusting object.

The only loophole is that no person shall be convicted if he establishes that the public good was served by what he did and that he did not go beyond the public good. The thorny problem of what exactly is the public good is determined by the judge. Whether the accused went beyond the public good is a question for the jury, or if there is no jury, the judge.

The good-hearted crusader who really believes that his magic cure will help millions of people is out of luck. The Code clearly states that the motives of the accused are irrelevant.

Not satisfied with federal authority in controlling questionable treatments for V.D., Saskatchewan has its own laundry list of prohibitions. It includes the publishing, issuing, posting, exhibiting, distributing, circulating, delivering or sending by post of any notice, advertisement, statement, testimonial, letter, book, almanac, pamphlet, fly sheet, document or other matter intended to recommend or suggest the purchase of or to promote the sale of any article as a drug, medicine, appliance or instrument or as part of any treatment for the alleviation or cure of venereal disease or of any disease of the genito-urinary organs, or intended to convey and offer to give or prescribe any form of treatment for any of the said diseases. If words can kill, the people of Saskatchewan are well protected.

Even this legislation has a loophole. It does not apply to any book, document, paper or other matter published in good faith for the advancement of medical or surgical science. It also does not apply to any article which has been approved by the Saskatchewan minister of public health. There is no appeal from his decision which may be based on anything he chooses.

To further put the cap on magical cures, the federal Food and Drug Act prohibits the labeling, packaging, treating, processing, selling or advertising of any drug or device in a manner that is false, misleading or deceptive, or is likely to create an erroneous impression. Therefore, condoms, which are often used to reduce the risk of V.D., are carefully labeled so as not to be passed off as fail-safe protection.

## The Root Cause

What is the answer? In attempting to control the spread of V.D., legislators first attempted to control the sexual act. This is obviously impossible. The power of the law can never extend to human conduct of such a personal nature. To pass laws against sexual activity is naive at best, and at worst, misleading to the public in suggesting that corrective action is being taken. Secondly, legislative attempts to control treatment have failed because of the social stigma surrounding V.D. and how it is contracted. Attempts to control the advertising of false treatments seem to have been effective, but have had no effect on reducing the spread of the disease itself. These latter two attempts are aimed solely at treating those who already have become infected. The first is aimed at prevention but, because of the nature of the disease, can never be effective.

The causes of the rising rate of V.D. must be examined. It is not due to any inherent or changing characteristic of the disease itself. Therefore, one can only theorize that more people are having sexual relations with multiple partners rather than exclusively with one person. Exclusivity in sexual relations, abstention and precautions such as the use of condoms are the only methods of reducing the spread of the disease. Law by its very nature does not touch individuals sufficiently on a personal basis to ensure that these methods are adopted.

The causes of the increase in indiscriminate sexual activity are as follows:

• Increased population mobility and migration result in contacts between people who do not know each other very well and in the increased need for personal contact, as people find themselves alienated in strange cities. Urbanization has also increased promiscuity. The social controls of the small town are gone. People in large cities do not know each other as well as do their country cousins. As a result, they are not in a position to pass judgment on the sexual experience of others. The impersonal nature of a city allows for more indiscriminate sexual activity than in a small town.

• Higher birth rates, at least in some areas, have increased the youthful and most sexually active part of the population. This means that a higher proportion of the public will be capable of promiscuity.

• Traditional value systems, which frown on extramarital and homo-sexual relations, have been discarded by many people. Although adhering to these systems did not prevent such relations from taking place, it at least discouraged them. These values are still held by a very large number of people, but in society as a whole, they are not as popular. The flaunting of these values is not as difficult as following them. In some circles it may even be encouraged. The lowering or even disappearance of previous religious, family and public restraints have also had an effect.

• It was the fear of unwanted pregnancy that prevented many in the past from having extramarital relations. With "the pill," many women no longer feel restrained. Knowing that women are protected from pregnancy, men often do not take precautions to prevent venereal disease and women do not insist that they do so. This lack of precaution may also be coupled with a general lack of knowledge about the risk of V.D., particularly among young people.

• Medicare coverage of V.D. treatment by private physicians rather than public clinics may also have contributed to the increased prevalence of the disease. Private physicians treat the patient, but usually do not report cases to public health officials, unlike the public clinics. As unsuccessful as the contact tracing may be, at least it is an attempt to break the chain of infection.

Discussions of the causes and the spread of V.D. are often attacked for being moralistic. V.D., it is said, could be attacked more successfully without a moralistic stigma. Such an accusation is a red herring. The morality of what people may be doing is a separate issue. The fact is that V.D. is a sexually transmitted disease. If people are going to have sexual relations with those who may have had relations with others infected with V.D., they are exposing themselves to the risk of infection. If they do not want to abstain from, or limit, their relations, they can only take precautions to reduce the risk by using condoms.

None of these causes can be affected by legislation. The answer is education. Health education for the public, however, receives low priority in all government health budgets. Perhaps society prefers it that way. Maybe society is unwilling to admit the real causes of the increase in V.D. Government advertisements urging teenage boys to wear condoms would serve as unpleasant reminders.

## Marriage, Crime and Venereal Disease

V.D. cannot be regarded simply as a health problem. It also has an effect on marriage and crime, and, as a result, on the law. In the 1943 Alberta case of *Loewen* v. *Loewen*, the wife sued her husband for divorce on the grounds of adultery. The couple had separated, but did stay together twice in a hotel during two successive months. The wife introduced evidence that the husband had venereal disease and asked the court to conclude that he had, therefore, committed adultery. The husband said that he got it from his wife. She, however, was found to be free of the disease. The court agreed with the woman and granted the divorce. The principle established in this case was that if a spouse had contracted V.D. which could not have come from the other spouse, the court is entitled to assume that it was contracted by adultery. It would be up to the infected party to prove that it was innocently contracted—undoubtedly a difficult task.

V.D. can also have an effect on the prosecution of a criminal offense. In 1888, the view was expressed by an English judge in the case of *R*. v. *Clarence* that a husband might be convicted of rape against his wife if he had intercourse with her maliciously, with the intent to give her V.D. Canada has never had such a case before its courts and probably never could, since rape is defined differently in this country than in England.

The fact that a person has V.D. may be used as evidence in support of a prosecution. A nine-year-old girl alleged that the accused had intercourse with her. This is a criminal offense because of her age. Soon after the offense was supposed to have occurred, she was medically examined and found to have venereal disease. The accused also was infected. While it does not necessarily follow that the girl was infected by the accused, the jury is entitled to consider this as a distinct possibility when it weighs all the evidence.

## "Thou art Rotted with the Pox"

Many public health officials advocate the social rehabilitation of people with V.D. Alcoholism, epilepsy, neurosis and leprosy are well on their way to losing much of their social stigma. Lepers no longer carry bells and cry "Unclean!" Alcoholics go to meetings, often attended by some of the most prominent people in society. In some circles, it is fashionable to have a neurosis.

The theory behind this movement in V.D. circles is that the stigma leads to secrecy and embarrassment. People delay in getting treatment. They are afraid to tell their spouses, their girlfriends and boyfriends that they have been infected. The spouses, girlfriends and boyfriends then unwittingly spread it to others. As shocking as this may seem to many from a moral point of view, it is the reality of the situation among a very large number of people and it must be faced.

Regardless of the argument as to how society should view venereal disease, the fact is that it is not socially acceptable to have it. This is reflected in the law of defamation dating back hundreds of years.

Defamation is a false statement, either written (called libel) or spoken (called slander), which exposes a person to hatred, ridicule or contempt, or which causes him to be shunned or avoided, or which might cause injury in his or her profession, office or trade. As far back as 1599, an English court in the case of *Davies* v. *Taylor* declared that the words "Thou art rotted with the pox" were defamatory. ("Pox" or "the French pox" means venereal disease.) This followed along the lines of *Austin* v. *White* in 1591 when it was decided that the words "Thou wert laid of the French pox" were actionable. This was confirmed throughout the years and was certainly not restricted to V.D. The words "Thou art a leprous knave" were considered actionable in 1607, in the case of *Taylor* v. *Perkins*.

There have been cases, however, where saying that someone has V.D. (when they do not) was not defamatory. In the 1788 case of *Carslake* v. *Mapledoram,* the words "I have kept her common these seven years, she hath given me the bad disorder, and three of four other gentlemen" were declared not actionable. The lady referred to could not take legal action since there was no reason why her company should be avoided. The public health officials would be delighted.

# 8 The Ladies (and Gentlemen) of the Night

The world's oldest profession is the most prosecuted. Western society has been passing laws against prostitutes for generations but continues to enjoy their services. The prostitute is harassed by police and driven from the streets. She is excluded from "polite" society at all social levels; yet politicians, doctors, lawyers, and archbishops enjoy her favors from coast to coast.

Why then is the legal system so vicious in its treatment of the prostitute? If the answer is morality, it is a weak excuse. Canada permits men to have sexual intercourse with one another and we permit the killing of unborn babies on the thinnest of criteria. We allow certain kinds of gambling, and films showing the most intimate of sexual pleasures. We allow our ambassadors and prime ministers to party with and give money to foreign leaders who torture, murder and permit the cutting off of hands as punishment. Some would say that these activities are just as immoral and destructive of social order as the payment by a client to a prostitute for pleasure and sexual companionship which the client cannot obtain within the traditional marriage setting.

The question to ask is whether Parliament is using the Criminal Code to enforce morality? Is it the role of the law to prevent individuals from providing sexual services to one another for payment if both parties are acting on their own free will and if no one is being injured?

Is it the role of law to control sexual promiscuity in exchange for money, when the law does not control promiscuity that has no financial strings attached? It can be argued that prostitution may be less harmful than nonfinancial extramarital sex which may carry serious emotional burdens. It has even been suggested that as society allows for greater sexual promiscuity outside of marriage with the weakening of social and religious restraints, prostitution will decrease. One wonders whether this is a socially desirable development.

The key problem behind all of these arguments is that prostitution exists throughout the world and has existed throughout history. According to A. A. Sion in his extensive study of *Prostitution and the Law* in England, "So long as the average human male is endowed with an imperative sexual urge that cannot be gratuitously satisfied and is economically in a position to provide some material reward in consideration for his sexual release, prostitution will inevitably exist."

There are four "evils" of prostitution which legal systems throughout the world have attempted to control: a) public indecency; b) public nuisance; c) the spread of venereal disease; and d) the possible adverse effect on children. Canadian law concentrates on public nuisance and the effect on children.

Traditionally, there have been three methods used by the legal systems of various countries to control prostitution. Some countries have attempted suppression or total prohibition of prostitution. This method requires prohibition of every act directly or indirectly involved in prostitution. The problem is that this method tends to drive prostitution underground and into criminal circles. It also increases the possibility of exploitation.

The second method is to admit that prostitution is a legal activity, but one that requires regulation. This includes licensing brothels and prostitutes, confining prostitutes to certain areas of the city, setting health standards and prohibiting prostitutes from entering certain public places. In practice this method has also failed. It is difficult to enforce and as a result is largely ignored.

The third method used by most countries, including Canada, is the abolition not of prostitution, but of the laws prohibiting it. Parliament admits that prostitution cannot be eradicated. It is believed that the more public aspects of it can be checked, however, including soliciting in public places, brothel-keeping and living off prostitution.

Admitting that prostitution is with us forever, or at least as long as there is a market for this service, Canada has attempted to control the more annoying features of the business. It has done this under the Criminal Code of Canada. The result is that the laws pertaining to prostitution are the same from coast to coast, unlike in the United States where the criminal law differs from state to state, or in the European Economic Community where each of the nine member states has a different law.

## The White Slave Trade

Prior to the rise of civil rights movements in the United States in the 1960s, it was felt that one of the great evils of civilized society was the abduction and selling of white women into prostitution. There was little concern about women of other colors.

On May 18, 1904, 13 countries signed an agreement in Paris for the repression of trade in white women. The British ambassador to France signed on behalf of His Majesty the King of the United Kingdom of Great Britain and Ireland and of the British Dominions beyond the Seas, Emperor of India. Thus Canada became a party to the agreement. Other countries were subsequently added, including the United States in 1908. This agreement was updated and revised and subsequently became The International Convention of the White Slave Traffic signed at Lake Success, New York, on May 4, 1949. At that time, Canada signed on its own behalf.

All signatories agreed to punish any person who, to gratify the passion of others, has hired, abducted or enticed, even with her consent, a woman or girl who is a minor, for immoral purposes; or by fraud, violence, threats, abuse of authority or constraint, abducted or enticed an adult woman or girl for immoral purposes, even when these various acts took place in different countries.

The Convention now bears the seal of the United Nations, but like so many other attempts to moralize the world, the trade in human beings, internationally and nationally, continues. Perhaps society likes it that way.

## The Crime of Soliciting

It may be a surprise to many Canadians that the actual act of prostitution, that is, sex for money, is not a crime in this country. Being a prostitute is also not a crime. What *is* a crime is "soliciting." The Criminal Code states in section 195.1, "Every person who solicits in a public place for the purpose of prostitution is guilty of an offense punishable on summary conviction."

The first question which the courts had to answer after this section was added in 1972 was, "what is meant by 'soliciting?'" On May 8, 1975 at 9:25 PM Detective Barclay of the Vancouver City Police sat casually dressed in street clothes in an unmarked car. He saw the accused, Hutt. She smiled at him. He smiled back. She approached the car, opened the door and got in. She asked him if he wanted a girl. He said, "Okay" and was told it would cost $30. She told him she was a prostitute. They went to the Dufferin Hotel where she was arrested.

The court determined that that officer's car was not a public place since the public would not ordinarily have access to it. But if the conversation had taken place on the sidewalk, would the woman's conduct have constituted "soliciting?" To answer this question, the Supreme Court of Canada had to determine what it was that Parliament intended by passing the law prohibiting soliciting. It was obviously not to outlaw prostitution. The law up to July 15, 1972 attempted to do that, and it was repealed. Until 1972, it was an offense to be a "common prostitute or nightwalker" who is found in a public place and is not able, when required, to give a good account of herself. A common prostitute was, according to Mr. Justice Johnson of the Saskatchewan Court of Queen's Bench, a woman who for payment offers herself to men generally, not merely to one or two.

The approach generally taken by the courts since 1972 allows prostitutes to be in public places but not to inconvenience the public or make a nuisance of themselves. It is not enough for a prostitute to make herself available for prostitution. She has to be persistent and annoying. She has to pressure the prospective client in order to be found guilty of soliciting. Not all judges agree with this interpretation of the law. In some cases prostitutes have been found guilty of soliciting simply by making themselves available for sex in return for money. Convictions for soliciting, however, are not exclusive to the prostitute. The potential customer could also be convicted of soliciting "in a public place for the purpose of prostitution." This was made clear by the Chief Justice of Ontario on August 8, 1978 in the case of *The Queen* v. *DiPaola*. In this case, it was reported that on December 7, 1977 DiPaola, a man of good character who was studying to become a teacher, stopped his car at the corner of Church and Isabella Streets in Toronto after circling the area. He honked the horn at a woman who ignored him and continued walking. He circled the area again, stopped and honked. The woman went over to the vehicle and asked if there was anything wrong. He asked her to get into the car but she refused. He asked her for a "French" kiss. She refused. He offered her $30 for an act of sexual intercourse. She entered the car and directed him to the rear of a building at 100 Wellesley Street. It was then that DiPaola discovered that his companion was a policewoman and he was arrested and convicted of soliciting.

The DiPaola case is important for it cleared the way for customers to be guilty of soliciting and it broadened the meaning of prostitution. The court said that prostitution was not to be limited to sexual intercourse. It also included the offering of a person's body for other sexual gratification or the performance of physical acts of indecency for the sexual gratification of others—all in return for payment.

The result of these decisions is that male prostitutes who solicit customers are equally as guilty as the ladies who do so. It matters little whether the potential customers are men or women. It also means that customers are as open to prosecution for soliciting as are the prostitutes themselves. This means that call girls or male companions are virtually free from prosecution as long as they do not solicit. Their customers may be in trouble.

## Support Services

Every business has surrounding it a number of other businesses which service it and depend on it for their support. The prostitution business is no different. The Criminal Code, while fairly lax in its attitude towards prostitutes, is severe in its condemnation of people who may not be prostitutes themselves but make their living from the prostitution business. It aims to protect prostitutes against pimps, madams and others who, as the Victorians would say, are "dealers in flesh." Unlike the sexual equality awarded to male prostitutes, however, insofar as soliciting is concerned, only female prostitutes are protected against exploitation by others.

Section 195 of the Code prohibits procuring or attempting to procure a woman for "illicit sexual intercourse with another person" or enticing her to, or concealing her in, a common bawdy-house. It prohibits any attempt to get women to go outside Canada to become prostitutes or direct women on arrival in Canada to houses of prostitution. It prohibits anyone from controlling a woman's movements or drugging her in order to carry on prostitution.

Only one part of section 195 attempts to protect male as well as female prostitutes. It prohibits anyone from living "wholly or in part on the avails of prostitution of another person." Because the section is designed to control the activities of people other than prostitutes, it is not illegal for the prostitute herself or himself to live wholly or in part on the avails of her or his own prostitution.

The more vicious activity of abduction is also included in the Criminal Code. It aims to punish with imprisonment of up to ten years anyone who takes away or detains a female against her will with intent to marry her or to have illicit sexual intercourse with her. It also punishes those who cause her to marry or to have illicit sexual intercourse with a male person. Boys who are abducted are not protected by this provision, though their abductors could be charged under the more general section dealing with kidnaping.

Girls under 16 are given special protection. If they are abducted from their parents or guardian, even if the girl consents or suggests it or if the abductor believes the girl is over 16, the penalty is a maximum of five years.

The Criminal Code does not limit its attacks to the managers and entrepreneurs of the prostitution industry. It also attacks those who provide transportation, not to a prostitute, but to "a common bawdy-house." Everyone who knowingly takes, transports, directs, or offers to take, transport, or direct any other person to a common bawdy-house is guilty of an offense. So much for late-night taxis. The key is, what is a common bawdy-house?

## The Bawdy-House

Nicole Sheehan lived in apartment 507 at 500 De Gaspé on Nun's Island, Montreal. She had two telephones, one of them for business and the other for an answering service. Miss Sheehan ran an advertisement in "Current Events," a magazine distributed in the rooms of many of the large hotels in Montreal. It read, "Lovely escort, help you enjoy Montreal, 789-4535."

When she received calls from gentlemen in response to the advertisement, she would tell the caller that her fee was $40 for two hours of female company. Financial arrangements for extra services would be made when the parties meet, she would say. She then made arrangements to meet her clients in hotel rooms. No sexual acts took place in Miss Sheehan's apartment and no discussion of sex ever took place over the telephone.

According to Mr. Justice Turgeon of the Quebec Court of Appeal, the object was to recruit clients for acts of prostitution, but that was not done at the apartment, nor over the telephone. For these reasons

Miss Sheehan was found not guilty of keeping a common bawdy-house.

A common bawdy-house, according to the Criminal Code, is a place that is kept, or occupied or resorted to by one or more persons for the purpose of prostitution or the practice of acts of indecency. The term "disorderly house" includes a common bawdy-house. The question is whether the so-called massage parlor is a common bawdy-house. If it clearly exists for the purpose of prostitution, the answer is yes. The difficulty is in proving it.

Following restrictions on soliciting and support services, the third restriction which the law places on the prostitution business is directed at the premises used for prostitution. It is an offense to keep a common bawdy-house, to be an "inmate" of one, to be found "without lawful excuse" in one, or to allow one's premises to be used as a common bawdy-house. A warrant may be issued to allow the police to enter and search any place which a policeman has reasonable grounds to believe or does believe is a common bawdy-house. The police may arrest everyone found on the premises. Warrants may also authorize searches for women enticed to, or concealed in, a common bawdy-house.

To bring about a conviction under this section of the Criminal Code, the Crown prosecutor must prove to the court that the premises were in frequent or habitual use for purposes of prostitution. A single act of prostitution in an apartment, house or hotel room does not turn the place into a common bawdy-house. The fact that one room in a hotel is used as a common bawdy-house does not turn the whole hotel into one. A prostitute, however, who regularly conducts her business in her own home, turns it into a common bawdy-house. The law is clearly directed at abolishing "houses of ill repute."

The logical conclusion is that Canada does not want to eradicate prostitution, but simply the showier aspects of it—soliciting, pimping and brothel-keeping. If a prostitute makes house-calls and does not solicit, the law is not concerned.

## Prostitution and Children

Canadian law may admit that prostitution cannot be totally wiped out, but it certainly is not about to encourage it. It may accept the fact that thousands of adults are engaged in the buying and selling of sexual services. The law, however, is not so tolerant about the involvement of children.

The Criminal Code makes it an offense for any parent or guardian to procure their daughter to have illicit sexual intercourse with a third party, or "orders, is party to, permits or knowingly receives the avails of, the defilement, seduction or prostitution" of their daughter. If the girl is under the age of 14, the offense carries a maximum penalty of 14 years' imprisonment. If she is over 14, the maximum penalty is five years. The parent or guardian of a son are not dealt with specifically under the Criminal Code.

Girls under 18 are also given protection. The owner, occupier or manager of premises who allow girls under 18 to be on the premises for the purpose of having "illicit sexual intercourse" are guilty of an offense. Boys do not receive the same protection. These offenses do not apply just to sex for money, but to sex generally, though one wonders what is meant by "illicit."

Girls are given special protection, but boys are not totally ignored by the Criminal Code. Everyone who, in the home of a child under the age of 18, "participates in adultery or sexual immorality or indulges in habitual drunkenness or any other form of vice, and thereby endangers the morals of the child or renders the home an unfit place for the child to be in" is liable to imprisonment for two years. This provision applies to both boys and girls.

To be valid, criminal proceedings taken under any of these provisions must be commenced within one year of the time the offense is alleged to have been committed.

## Contracts with Prostitutes

Movies and literature have glamorized the prostitute—the sideways glance, the tight sweater, the raised skirt; the sailor, the soldier, the businessman slumming—it has all the elements of a novel. It is a one-time fling, as the boy is initiated into manhood or the man becomes a boy for a fleeting moment. It may not be socially acceptable, but it is at least tolerated.

What is not tolerated is the regular customer. The regular customer may want a standing arrangement on a contractual basis. The pimp may also want a contract. The taxi driver may also prefer a contract to provide transportation to the brothel rather than depend upon haphazard customers.

If any of these contracts comes into question and any of the parties takes legal action to obtain payment or services due, the courts will not support the contract. As far back as 1793, Chief Justice Lord Kenyon said that the law will not enforce a contract which is against good morals. Even if the object of the contract was not illegal, the courts would not stand behind it because it is immoral.

## What is Immorality?

Throughout any study of the law related to prostitution the words "immoral," "illicit" and "indecent" are referred to constantly. These terms are used in the Criminal Code and in court decisions. One wonders what these words really mean. References by the courts to "the rules and principles of morality," "public welfare" and "community standards" are not very helpful.

There can never be an exact definition of immorality. In Canada's diversified society of the 1980s, what is immoral according to one sector of society is not to another. The role of the judge and of the law is to reflect society. It is often difficult to know what the average Canadian, or Canadian society as a whole, feels. When it comes to making a decision on such unclear and controversial issues, the judge will determine morality and immorality either as he or she views it or as the judge thinks society in general views it. No more scientific method has been found.

## The Enigma

The legal problems facing prostitutes and the prostitution business go on and on. If society gives up the battle to rid itself of a business which it really wants and concentrates only on the exploitation of people against their will, the legal problems will be similar to those affecting the rest of society.

If a customer is injured by a prostitute or vice versa, can the injured party sue? Can the dissatisfied customer get his money back? Can the prostitute collect unsatisfied debts from customers on credit? Will we see houses of prostitution with red lights flickering on a small sign in the window stating, "All major credit cards accepted?"

# 9  Rape and Sexual Assault

## Protection of the Body

There is nothing like a good rape or an indecent assault to set tongues a-wagging. It is the highlight of books and films. It sells newspapers and magazines. It is publicized or it is actively suppressed, but never ignored. The public is shocked and they love it. The courtrooms are sold out.

Cloaked with the aura of academia, psychiatrists and psychologists deliciously study the rapist and his victim. Learned theories are developed about sexual suppression, inferiority complexes and mother-son relationships. Women's liberationists explain rape and indecent assault in terms of a male plot designed to terrorize the entire female population into submission.

The taboos, the fears, the misconceptions and the curiosity about these two crimes have crept into Canadian law. As public attitudes slowly change, Parliament changes the Criminal Code, but both move slowly. Radical changes, which would remove even the word *rape* from the legal vocabulary, have been proposed by the Law Reform Commission of Canada. At the time of this writing, however, Parliament has taken no action. Rape and indecent assault are not priority issues with the public and therefore not with Parliament.

In its attempt to maintain a minimum level of social order and stability, the law has long prohibited citizens from interfering with one another's bodies. The law gives the victim the right to sue his or her attacker. Freedom from bodily assault is regarded as being so important that the victim can sue even though he has not suffered any physical injuries.

Assaults between citizens not only hurt the victims. The community as a whole is affected by encouraging the settling of all disputes by assault. It encourages lawlessness, terrorism and social disintegration. The solution is not simply to allow victims to sue. The state has had to step in.

When it steps in, the state never does so in a simple, straightforward manner. It establishes a system of categories, procedures and exceptions. In attempting to control an otherwise unruly populace from assaulting one another, the state—and through it the law—does just that. It is not enough to prevent assault. People have the feeling that some assaults are more serious than others and that the state should try a little harder to prevent some attacks more than others. When it fails to prevent assaults, society wants to protest some assaults more vigorously than others by punishing the attackers more severely.

The following chart illustrates how the Canadian law in the Criminal Code ranks assault in terms of punishment for crimes against the person:

1. $500 maximum, or six months' imprisonment or both
   - *common assault*
2. Five years maximum
   - *assault causing bodily harm* • *assault to unlawfully retain property* • *assault to resist arrest* • *assault to commit an indictable (serious) offense* • *indecent assault on a female*
3. Ten years maximum
   - *indecent assault on a male by another male* • *indecent assault on anyone by a male with intent to commit buggery (i.e. sodomy)* • *attempted rape* • *rape* • *criminal negligence causing bodily harm* • *criminal negligence causing death*
4. Maximum life imprisonment
   - *manslaughter*
5. Mandatory life imprisonment
   - *murder*

Abolished: • *whipping* • *execution*

In theory, the legal position is, as Gilbert and Sullivan's "Mikado" put it, "Let the punishment fit the crime!" It does not fit the criminal, nor does it fit the victim. Some women may be psychologically damaged for life from an indecent assault, whereas other women may recover from the shock of being raped. The law views rape as more serious, however, and therefore imposes a greater penalty.

The relative seriousness of the various types of assault may seem peculiar to many. Indecent assault on a male is regarded as far more serious than indecent assault on a female since the maximum penalty is twice as great, except in cases of buggery. Considering the economic and political problems facing this country, the public is not about to push government and Parliament into readjusting the law of assault.

The laws of assault clearly show that society is obsessed with sex. It values sex more than almost anything else. In examining the list of crimes against the person, one can see that sex added to violence moves assault up to near the top of the imprisonment list. Only the life of a person is more highly protected in terms of punishment.

## Indecent Assault

The moralist may say that any assault on the body of another person is indecent, but not so in law. It is sex that turns assault into indecent assault. To obtain a conviction of assault without sex, the Crown prosecutor must prove to the court that the accused either touched the victim or attempted or threatened to touch the victim. The Crown must also prove that the victim reasonably believed that the assault would take place. There need not have been any bodily contact for an assault; the threat is sufficient. Nor is it necessary for the victim to have suffered any harm. It is necessary, however, to prove that whatever happened was not consented to by the victim.

There are cases in which the victim has consented and the accused was still convicted. These are in circumstances when the consent was obtained, in the words of the Criminal Code, "by false and fraudulent representations as to the nature and quality of the act."

In the 1967 Ontario Court of Appeal case of *The Queen* v. *Maurantonio*, the victim consented to medical examinations by the accused who had falsely held himself out as a doctor to about 200 female patients and 20 male patients. He did in fact perform an examination on each of them, but since he was not a doctor, the court said that he really did not perform a "medical" examination. The victims were therefore subjected to something entirely different from that to which they had consented. The "doctor" was convicted of indecent assault.

In the same year, a real doctor from British Columbia found himself before the Supreme Court of Canada on a charge of indecent assault. Dr. Bolduc was accompanied by his friend, Bird, who was up on the same charge. Dr. Bolduc was to examine a female patient. Over the protests of his receptionist, he gave his friend, Bird, a white lab coat and took him into the examining room. Dr. Bolduc introduced his friend as "Dr. Bird," an intern. In fact, "Dr." Bird was a night club musician who wanted to go to medical school.

Dr. Bolduc did a careful examination of his patient's private parts while Bird stood by watching, never speaking and never touching. The question facing the court was whether either of them was guilty of indecent assault. After all, the patient had consented to the examination by a doctor and had received exactly that. The court expressed its shock at Dr. Bolduc's "unethical and reprehensible" conduct. Did this, however, make the patient's consent invalid? Was her consent obtained "by false and fraudulent representations as to the nature and quality of the act?" The answer was "no." While there was fraud as to Bird being a medical intern, Bolduc only said that he would observe, which is what he did. Bird did not touch, therefore, no assault. Bolduc did what was consented to, therefore, no assault on his part.

It is possible for an act which is not indecent to be considered indecent when the court examines all of the surrounding circumstances. The facts of a case may turn an ordinary assault into an indecent one. When a 51-year-old man enticed a nine-year-old girl in a white communion dress into a cubicle of a men's washroom, put his hands on her stomach and back and tried to pull down her pants— according to the Ontario Court of Appeal, it was indecent assault, even though he never actually assaulted her. It is not the part of the body touched which makes the act indecent. It is the attacker's obvious intent to do something indecent that counts. If the attacker does touch a part of the body obviously associated with sex, the court can assume that the intent was indecent assault.

Not only must the accused have physical contact with the victim or threaten it, there must be some aggressive act by the accused. A mere request does not constitute indecent assault. When Mr. Baney took out his penis in front of a four-year-old boy and asked him to play with it, no indecent assault was committed—according to the Ontario Court of Appeal in 1971. He did not touch, attempt or threaten, by any act or gesture to apply force. The boy, as it turned out, refused. In some cases children can protect themselves better than adults.

## Rape

Moving up the ladder from indecent assault on a female are the more serious offenses, according to law, of indecent assault on a male, attempted rape and rape. Even though the punishment can be greater for indecently assaulting a male than a female, the law surrounding the crime is the same. The law relating to rape and attempted rape is quite different.

The Criminal Code defines the offense of rape as sexual intercourse by a man with a woman who is not his wife without her consent or when her consent is extorted, obtained by impersonating her husband or "is obtained by false and fraudulent representations as to the nature and quality of the act."

The striking features of this law are:

* Only a man can be found guilty of rape. A woman who forces a man to have sexual intercourse with her may be guilty of a lesser crime of indecent assault, but not of rape. A woman can only be found guilty of rape if she was a party to it; that is, aided or abetted the rape of another woman.

* Only a woman can be raped. Homosexual gang "rape," which is supposed to be a feature of prison life, is not legally rape, though it is indecent assault.

* A man cannot by law rape his own wife. He can force her to have sexual intercourse, which may be common assault or even indecent assault, but not rape. The theory is that by marrying, she has consented to intercourse "till death do us part." Even if they are separated, the husband cannot be convicted of raping his wife. They would have to be divorced.

* A man can only be found guilty of rape on his own wife if he was party to someone else raping her.

* No one under 14 years of age can be found guilty of rape or attempted rape, regardless of what he did.

The dividing line between indecent assault and rape is drawn around what some have called society's interest in protecting the sanctity of the vagina. It is sexual intercourse which turns indecent assault into rape. To make certain that everyone knows what sexual intercourse means, section 3(6) of the Criminal Code tells us, "...(S)exual intercourse is complete upon penetration to even the slightest degree, notwithstanding that seed is not emitted." A British

Columbia County Court in the 1956 case of *The Queen* v. *Johns* added to the definition by saying that sexual intercourse during rape was also achieved even if the hymen was not touched or the vagina was not penetrated. The conclusion is that the unsuccessful lover may become a convicted rapist.

## Defense to a Charge of Rape

The major defense to a charge of rape, assuming that sexual intercourse did take place, is that of consent. If the defense can show that the victim consented to the intercourse, the accused must be found not guilty.

The question of whether the victim consented will always come down to the question of who is lying the least, the victim or the accused. It was thought at one time that an accused could not be convicted unless there was evidence in addition to that of the victim's testimony.

Today an accused can be found guilty on the victim's evidence alone, but the judge may warn the jury that it would be very dangerous to do this. Finding other evidence, particularly witnesses, is difficult.

Consent may be obtained by threats either to the victim or to another person such as her husband, parent or child. In the eyes of the law, this is no consent at all, and it fails in the defense of the accused. What is not clear is whether the accused rapist is not guilty if he was forced to rape the victim because of threats to himself. Such a defense is ordinarily allowed by the Criminal Code if the potential violence was carried out by someone present. However, this defense does not apply in cases of "assisting in rape" and "causing bodily harm."

The accused may also defend himself if he has an honest but mistaken belief that the victim was in fact consenting. The difficulty is presenting sufficient evidence to support such a defense.

## Sex by Fraud

Consent to intercourse may be invalidated if it was obtained by false and fraudulent representations as to the nature and quality of the act. It follows the words of the law on indecent assault.

The Saskatchewan Court of Appeal faced this problem in the 1943 case of *The King* v. *Harms*. Ruth Clarke had been suffering a pain in her chest and was advised by her father to see the accused who was known as Dr. Harms. Harms was no doctor and "practised" in a rooming house over a café in Melfort, Saskatchewan.

At about midnight on August 14, 1942 Ruth Clarke visited Harms in his lodgings. He had her drink a tumbler of yellow liquid which he described as "just a couple of pills." He had her lie down, removed her undergarment and inserted two pills in her private parts. He removed his own underpants and got on her, saying that he was doing it to make the pills operative. As he put it, "She would have to get hot and bothered." The girl objected but was finally convinced that her cooperation was necessary if the treatment was to be effective. On June 3, 1943 Ruth Clarke gave birth. The jury concluded that her consent was obtained "by false and fraudulent representations as to the nature and quality of the act." Harms' conviction was upheld on appeal.

## "Violated in her Slumber"

As described in Brecht's *Three Penny Opera*, there have been a number of cases considered by the courts in which a woman was raped in her sleep. Can it then be described as rape since the victim did not protest? The law was set out in the 1872 Manchester, England case of *The Queen* v. *Mayers,* by Mr. Justice Lush, stating "...[If] a man gets into bed with a woman while she is asleep, and he knows she is asleep and he has connection with her, or attempted to do so while in that state, he is guilty of rape in the one case and the attempt in the other."

The same logic applies to a woman whose inebriation made it impossible for her to resist. Rape can be committed even if the victim did not resist. To say otherwise would allow the rapist to knock out his victim and, without her resistance, have sex with her without it being rape.

## A Wolf in Sheep's Clothing

On February 2, 1878 at 4:00 A.M., Johanna Hurley, her husband and their two children were all in bed together in their lodgings at the Seven Dials Inn. The accused entered the unlocked room, joined the four in the bed, and proceeded to have sex with Johanna who was asleep at the time. When she awoke she thought it was her husband until she heard him speak and noticed her husband by her side. Her lack of consent made this clearly a case of rape. She was asleep and did not consent.

If, however, a man impersonates a married woman's boyfriend, obtains her consent and makes love to her, her consent is valid. She has consented to an extramarital affair and the law cares little about with whom it is performed.

## Wine, Women and Wine

An often heard defense to a charge of rape is drunkenness. Again and again the courts have said, "Drunkenness is no defense." This rule applies to both rape and indecent assault. In many of these cases, the accused was so drunk that he was never able to commit rape but got only as far as indecent assault. In all of these cases, however, the accused knew what he was doing.

Such was the case on November 29, 1968 when the naked Mr. Pharo chased after the then-clothed cleaning lady, Mrs. Horvath, in his St. Clair Avenue apartment in Toronto. Having forcibly removed her clothes, he kissed her private area and after some wrestling around on the dining room floor he massaged her breasts. His early morning liquor did not save him from conviction for indecent assault.

It also did not save Mr. Leary who, in a drunken state in Nelson, British Columbia, forced his victim at knife point to submit to coitus and other acts of sexual humiliation.

## A Tainted Lady

Unlike most other crimes, rape can be transformed into something noncriminal and pleasurable. All it takes is consent. On the occasion in question the victim is saying that she did not consent. How are the judge and jury to believe her? If it is known that she often had extramarital sex, why should the court believe that this occasion was any different? Why is she all of a sudden crying "Rape!?"

Prior to the mid-70s, defense lawyers made it a practice to attack the victim who appeared as a witness in a rape trial with respect to her sexual history. The purpose was to damage her credibility, so that no judge or jury would believe that her cry of "foul" was for real. This technique served to transfer the attention of the court onto the victim and off the accused. She, in effect, was being put on trial. As a result, many victims refused to be put through such an ordeal and prosecutions could not proceed.

On the other hand, the defendant may have been falsely accused and had to have an opportunity to defend himself by questioning his accuser. A compromise was reached with an amendment to the Criminal Code. It provides that no question shall be asked by or on behalf of the accused as to the sexual conduct of the complainant (victim) with a person other than the accused. The only exception to this rule is if the judge determines that the question is necessary to make a just determination, including whether the complainant can be believed. To obtain the judge's permission to do this, the lawyer for the accused has to be able to convince the judge that the failure to ask the question would seriously jeopardize his ability to defend the accused.

As a further test of whether the woman is telling the truth when she says she really did not consent, she must show the court that she complained at the first reasonable opportunity. If she waited before going to the police, she must be able to give some reasonable explanation for the delay. Even if she did delay, it does not mean that she is now lying, but it does raise suspicions.

## Extra! Extra!

If the public loves a good rape, then a rape trial is even better. The victim may be ruined by the publicity, as may the accused found not guilty. Canada, however, has a tradition of open, public trials to avoid the secretive and suspicious nature of trials in countries like the USSR. In balancing the two principles, the Criminal Code has favored the protection of the innocent over the public's right to know.

For this reason, the judge at a rape trial may exclude the public from the courtroom if he is "of the opinion that it is in the interest of public morals, the maintenance of order or the proper administration of justice." The judge also has the power to order that the identity of the complainant and her evidence shall not be published or broadcast.

## The Challenge

Despite all the discussion about sexual promiscuity, rape and indecent assault remain grave social problems causing concern and fear throughout the country. In recent years, many efforts have been made to minimize the risk of being raped. Women have been taught how to protect themselves if they are attacked and how to speak with the would-be rapist. Television, radio and the press have carried messages warning women not to walk alone in poorly lit areas or in areas known to be crime-ridden. Despite these preventive measures rape remains a serious criminal statistic.

Efforts have also been made to aid rape victims. Many large, urban hospitals now have specially trained staff to treat the rape victim. Special evidence kits are often available from police for physicians treating rape victims. These will aid in prosecuting the attacker.

Individual and group counseling are also available to help the woman work out the emotional shock and insult of the attack.

It is comforting to know that preventive steps are available to reduce the chance of being sexually assaulted. It is good to know that special treatment may be available for the victim of an indecent assault or a rape. The challenge, however, remains to wipe out completely both types of unwanted sexual activity.

Laws can be tightened up and penalties increased to thwart the sex offender, but the law alone cannot prevent a rape or an indecent assault. Growing public concern and awareness of violent sexual assaults are good indicators that the challenge to solve this serious social problem is yet to be met.

# 10 Sex Discrimination and Human Rights

Since the end of World War II, there has been much publicity over what has been labeled "human rights." What is not always clear is what the phrase means. What is even less clear is what it has to do with sex.

For a number of years human rights were associated with the Geneva Convention, that international agreement which was supposed to place certain limits on warfare and the holding of prisoners of war. With the discovery of the Nazi death camps, it was recognized that international conventions were not totally effective.

Human rights legislation, however, is not a recent phenomenon. The Ten Commandments relating to human life is a prime example of early law. It was followed by England's Magna Carta and that same country's Bill of Rights in 1688, the American Constitution and its Bill of Rights in 1791.

In the 20th century, human rights have been associated with Central American political killings, torture in South America, brainwashing in North Korea, confinement of dissidents in Soviet mental hospitals and mass murders by Americans in Vietnam. With the cries for racial equality in the American South, in Rhodesia (now Zimbabwe) and in South Africa, however, human rights took on an additional meaning beyond the right to be free from political murder and torture. They included the desire of people to be treated on the basis of their individual merits regardless of race, creed, color, religion or political beliefs and regardless of whether they are men or women. The cry was against the barriers, sometimes blatant, like the "White Only" signs in South African or Alabama hotels. Sometimes the barriers were subtle and more difficult to overcome.

The world was younger and more naive than it is today. People still believed in the United Nations. The UN took a stand and passed "The Universal Declaration of Human Rights." Member nations recognized that there had been a denial of basic human rights far beyond the right to life and liberty. There was racial, sexual, linguistic, religious and political inequality. This situation remains to this day. The UN pronouncement was a failure. Most nations have not been able to guarantee even the most basic rights—racial, religious, political or sexual.

## What are "Human Rights?"

This is a catchall phrase, elusive of definition and precise description. It has been, however, the subject of court decisions and legislative enactments going back to biblical times. These bills, charters and codes are nothing more than laundry lists of rights that have been established by various countries, parliaments and assemblies, which are so fundamental, that they cannot be altered by governments or by the courts. These lists differ from place to place and from generation to generation. These are rights a particular society felt were so important as to be labeled "human rights." What is included in the list in one place may not be elsewhere. Unless a particular desire is included in the list, it cannot be said to be a human right.

To a large extent, therefore, the subject "human rights" and its first cousin "civil liberties" is more important as a list of aspired-to goals, than as one of acknowledged rights. Many of these goals deal with fairness, understanding and compassion, none of which can be enforced by law. The more blatant abuse of human rights, that is, the denial of equality, has been dealt with in legislation.

Every province in Canada and the federal Parliament have passed a human rights act. While the federal law applies only to the conduct of federal activities, the provincial laws affect the activities of everyone else within provincial boundaries. This means that while the laws are very similar, what is meant by human rights in British Columbia may differ from what is meant by human rights in Newfoundland. Even where the words of the law are the same, the interpretation may be different. The law may also be enforced differently. It is clear that under the Canadian federal system, human rights, like education and health, are provincial matters. Therefore, human rights relating to sex, and perhaps even sex itself, are provincial.

Rights that are included in any human rights acts are really only a very small proportion of the rights which Canadians enjoy. Most rights are those held by Canadians under the traditions of the English Common Law in all provinces and territories outside Quebec and under the Civil Code in Quebec. These include the right to remain free from assault, trespass and defamation. These rights are enforced by individuals taking legal action to obtain compensation against others whom they accuse of interfering with their rights.

Canadians have essential rights to a fair trial, and the right to be convicted of a criminal offense only if the prosecution can prove their guilt beyond a reasonable doubt. These rights are protected by the Criminal Code of Canada. There are virtually hundreds of other federal and provincial laws, which give to Canadians their human rights, but which are not included in human rights legislation. These rights are the fundamental rights of any civilized society. Such rights are still lacking in most countries in the world.

Human rights, in the Canadian sense, do not deal with the essential rights, which are taken for granted in this country. Human rights legislation was developed to give protection against unequal treatment by Canadians of other Canadians when the basis of the unequal treatment was not reasonable and no longer considered socially proper, in other words—discrimination.

## Provincial Human Rights Laws

Provincial human rights acts are designed to eliminate discrimination on the basis of such factors as religion, physical handicap, ancestry, creed, color, nationality, age, marital status, race, political affiliation and sex. The laws touch everything from housing, hotel accommodations, employment, buying and selling property and trade unions, to wages and professional associations. On paper, these rights represent a glowing testimonial to the great push for human rights and dignity throughout Canada. In practice, and upon closer reading, the glow is considerably diminished. Nowhere is this more striking than in the area of sex.

In every province, the laws begin by banning discrimination on the basis of sex. The prohibition extends from trade unions that would exclude women or men, to corporations that would not hire women. It affects those selling property who would deny people of either sex the opportunity of buying land. It also prevents property owners from imposing conditions of sale that discriminate on the basis of sex. Landlords are prevented from denying commercial and residential space to people simply because they are men or women. It insists on equal wages for the same work, for men and women. On billboards, on television and radio or in newspapers and magazines, the laws prevent ads that even by implication restrict services or jobs to members of only one sex. Professional organizations are also affected in that they cannot deny qualified persons membership in the group on the basis of sex. Almost all aspects of life are covered.

## The Human Rights Commission

In each province and at the federal level, a human rights commission has the responsibility of enforcing its own human rights acts. Each commission also has the important task of promoting a better understanding of human rights.

Complaints are made to the commission which attempts to bring together the complaining party and the person against whom the complaint is made in the hope of reaching a settlement. If this cannot be accomplished, the commission can recommend that a board of inquiry be convened to explore the complaint in greater detail. A hearing is usually held in which testimony is given and documentary evidence is reviewed. The board, following its consideration of the evidence, passes along to the commission recommendations for resolving the dispute. The commission, in turn, may order an employer to reinstate an employee wrongfully dismissed on the basis of discrimination and it may order compensation, including lost wages. Similarly, in the case of housing or public accommodations discrimination, the commission may order that the person denied his rights be given such opportunities and privileges as are necessary to make up for previous violations of his or her rights. Failure to comply with a human rights act or with an order from a human rights commission may also trigger the imposition of fines. These range from as little as $100 to $2,000 for individuals and from $300 to $5,000 for corporate and association violators. The amount of the fine varies from province to province.

Each act also allows for appeal to a court of the commission's actions. In most instances, the highest court of the province is given the responsibility of hearing these appeals from provincial commissions. Appeals from the federal Human Rights Commission are made to a review tribunal. Under some human rights acts, the court may either approve the commission's decision or it may declare it unsuitable and substitute its own. The prospect of a court nullifying the commission's decision is quite slim, however, particularly when the commission has followed the laws governing its authority.

With ten provincial human rights commissions and one federal counterpart, what has been accomplished in the area of sex discrimination? Put another way, what *can* be done under the present laws?

## Impact of Human Rights Laws

It is impossible to change the course of social history overnight, to undo all the accepted customs and mores of Western culture. In the eyes of many, men and women are not equal. To change the obvious and the subtle forms of sexual discrimination in Canada today will take more than a "community awareness day" here, or a regulation there. Advertisements with hidden messages or job descriptions, which are skilfully worded to eliminate or at least discourage one sex or the other, are still very apparent.

Noncommercial "messages" in films, the press, television and literature continue to reinforce society's attitude that men and women are not interchangeable in jobs, housing and education. It may be impossible for human rights commissions to alter the attitudes developed by a society over hundreds of years.

Human rights legislation has been successful to some extent, however, in redressing some of the more blatant discriminatory practices. Significant inroads have been made. Women are now able to obtain jobs in areas previously barred to them in such industries as construction and in the military. Less social stigma is attached to men becoming "house-husbands," reversing the old established notion that the wife should remain at home and tend to domestic needs. Gradually, the categories of "women only" and "men only" are disappearing. Part of the change can be attributed to economic pressures, the women's liberation movement, and a better appreciation of the capabilities of people of both sexes. It is difficult to estimate how much of the new philosophy of the sexes can be credited to inroads made by human rights commissions. Much depends on the authority given to the commissions by legislation.

For example, Saskatchewan has clearly allowed its commission broad powers by defining sex to include pregnancy and pregnancy-related illnesses. The result is that discrimination against a woman because she is pregnant is just as unlawful as discrimination against her because she is a woman. Other provinces, in not defining "sex" for purposes of their human rights laws, may or may not prohibit such discrimination.

Employees denied advancement or paid at different rates for the same work on the basis of sex may be reluctant to initiate a complaint with a provincial human rights commission. They may fear reprisals or "blackballing" from further employment in the industry. To overcome this fear, a number of provinces have made it easier to file complaints. Some allow other persons to start the process, as long as they have permission to do so from the person who suffered the discrimination. Many human rights commissions may also initiate an investigation on their own. In other provinces such as Saskatchewan and Alberta, the human rights laws have built-in buffers which prevent employers from punishing an employee for starting or participating in a human rights proceeding. Thus, an employee cannot be fired, coerced or intimidated on this basis, nor can he or she be made to suffer any financial loss for doing so.

Even with these added safeguards, however, there are many drawbacks to the current style of human rights laws regarding sex discrimination. In large measure, the problem involves vaguely written exceptions which allow sex discrimination to continue in certain cases. "Bona fide occupational qualification" and "for the maintenance of public decency" are common exceptions to laws prohibiting discrimination on the basis of sex. No Canadian human rights law, however, defines what constitutes a "bona fide qualification" or "public decency." This has been left to either the regulations or the commissions to decide in individual cases. The exceptions were originally placed in the law so that advertising agencies would not be required to consider men and women on an equal basis when hiring models to display women's dresses, and so that theater companies could discriminate legally against actresses when casting for the part of King Lear. The exception on public decency also allowed the YMCA to hire only males as men's locker room attendants.

The absence of uniform criteria is not necessarily a bad feature, since the flexibility left in the application of the laws means that what is and is not discriminatory depends on the circumstances and social environment of each case. The problem with a lack of uniformity is that there may be unequal application of the law. Although some people may suffer an unfair decision as a result, it does not allow commissions the opportunity to tailor-make their recommendations in each case. For would-be victims of discrimination it means a "wait and see" approach to their complaints.

The question which arises from these limitations is whether the exceptions nullify the whole purpose of the human rights law. There is no evidence that this is the case. Depending on the attitude of each commission and the types of cases which come before them for consideration, however, it is possible that the exceptions can be used to blunt the full force of the legislation. Because the human rights commissions are political institutions, they cannot help but be influenced by the social and cultural environment in which they operate.

## Is Discrimination a Good Thing?

Even if qualifications are permitted on the basis of sex, one must ask: is it necessarily a bad thing? Are there not certain factors or situations which point towards needed distinctions based on sex?

If it is agreed that some allowance must be made on the basis of sex, the problem is where to draw the line. In most Canadian human rights laws there are specific provisions allowing discrimination. In housing accommodation, the owner of the two-unit dwelling in which he and his family reside may restrict occupancy of the other unit on the basis of sex. Similarly, if a family is renting out one room in their home, they can limit the potential list of renters to persons of one sex. The same restrictions would not be permitted in the renting of units in an apartment building.

Where the legislation permits the commissions to draw exceptions, as in employment, the fear is that they will release a watershed of sexual biases, but there may be good arguments in support of discrimination. Health of female workers is a good example. In many industries, exposure to chemicals and low-level amounts of radiation could pose a serious hazard to women in terms of their reproductive capacity. It could mean spontaneous miscarriages or serious birth defects for their offspring, or the risk of cancer to the women themselves. To avoid these problems and possible legal ramifications, employers either refuse to hire women altogether or hire them for work in less hazardous settings, such as the typing pool. The fact that men may also suffer adverse consequences from such exposure—including sterility or damaged sperm—seems to have been overlooked in the argument.

With public pressure from women's rights organizations and unions, it is doubtful that the human rights commissions would ever give their approval to blatant sex discrimination. This is particularly true in the case of "bona fide" occupational requirements. Employers may even be forced to clean up the work setting to make it safe for women or to show why this cannot be accomplished. In the process, the health and safety of male employees may also be improved.

## Maintenance of Public Decency

A more difficult matter is how to interpret the other type of exception based on sex, which is for the "maintenance of public decency." What does it mean? How does it relate to sex discrimination? When can it be legitimately used?

Unlike the bona fide employment qualifications, which at least can be quantified occasionally, there is no way to accurately gauge public decency. As complaints come before human rights commissions based on this exception, they must assess society's mood and moral expectations towards the integration of the sexes. It may be a matter of women sharing the same washroom with men at a work site, the presence of women at an all-men's swimming club or the renting of commercial space to two men who intend to operate a massage parlor in a shopping center. The cases may be more difficult, such as the employment of nursing mothers in a job setting where there is a lack of private quarters to feed their babies.

Applying this standard is a difficult task. The language of the exception is so vague and lacking in standards of application that the decision-makers could easily fall into the trap of applying subjective criteria. It is a distinction based on sex that is not static, but changes as society changes. The problem is that a new complaint or a new inquiry must be launched each time a person feels that the public decency qualification is no longer a valid reason to discriminate. Each commissioner's biases and upbringing will color his or her thinking. Without some minimum standards by which to consider each case, and without some idea of what the provincial assembly meant by "public decency" in the legislation, the commissioners have no alternative but to rely upon their own resources. Subjectivity and lack of standards could turn the "public decency" exception into a shield for discriminatory practices. While this is a legal possibility, one must also examine what is actually happening across Canada.

A young woman accompanied by a male friend went to a licensed tavern for a drink. They moved to a different table in the tavern to get away from the noisier part of the establishment. At this table the couple were denied service as they were told by a waiter it was the "men only" section. The next day, the young woman contacted the Ontario Human Rights Commission. She was told that it was unlawful to designate a "men only" section of the tavern. Acting upon the Commission's advice, she returned to the establishment ten days later to see if the previous encounter was a misunderstanding or an established policy. She and a woman companion took seats at a table in the same location. A waiter came by and told them to move to another area as this one was for men only. When they refused, the manager came over and told them to move. He pointed out that he would not tolerate them sitting in close proximity to the men's washroom since they "could watch men take whizzes in the washroom."

After an investigation and a hearing, the Human Rights Commission determined that the tavern was in violation of the Ontario Human Rights Act, even though the manager had based his decision on a genuine concern for the well-being of female patrons. There had been reports made to him of foul language and fighting which had disturbed some women. While appreciative of the manager's concerns, the Ontario Human Rights Commission stated that there was no justification for this type of sex discrimination. The exception based on "public decency" was not applicable. As the Commission stated, public decency refers to such things as separate washrooms and bath facilities, swimming pools and saunas. It does not provide a justification for segregated sections within a public tavern.

What could and does happen with the "maintenance of public decency" qualification are two different matters. As seen in the Ontario case, the human rights commissions are painfully aware of the broad latitude of the escape clause. Being so conscious of its detrimental potential, the commissions are loath to invoke it, and if they must, it is done in a very detailed and as objective a fashion as possible. The exception is usually narrowly drawn and the subject of strict scrutiny. The commissions are not completely without legal limits. Their actions are subject to review by the courts. It is nonetheless disturbing to many to have such broadly written exceptions to a law designed to eliminate sex discrimination.

## How Discrimination is Defined

With all the discussion of human rights and commissions empowered to prevent discrimination, what is meant by "discrimination?" Where is sex discrimination likely to occur? What are the policies underlying such activity? Do the Canadian human rights laws prevent sex discrimination in practice?

There is no doubt that blatant sex discrimination has been recognized and reduced in Canada. Employers are now forced to at least advertise job openings for men and women. Pay must be equal for equal work. Inequalities may remain for a long time, but a beginning has been made.

It is the subtle form of discrimination which is more difficult to identify and eliminate. In the employment field, it occurs by setting standards which on the surface apply to everyone, but which in fact keep out women. These standards often are not essential to the job itself.

For example, in the employment of women as police officers, local government officials may set a minimum height requirement of 5'4" for men and women alike. The fact that most women would be unable to meet this standard while most men would do so, is not in itself evidence of discrimination. The "impact" of the requirement, however, is to deny most women constable status. The underlying "purpose"—given the record of female employment in law enforcement— is likely discriminatory.

Discrimination is part of Canadian life, although it may not be as obvious and far-reaching as that found in the United States or in the United Kingdom.

## Where Does Sex Discrimination Occur?

Sex discrimination takes place in almost every aspect of Canadian life. It takes place in housing, public places, private clubs, business associations, employment, sports and education. It involves bias against men and women alike. It varies from the blatant, overt variety to the subtle. Some of the discrimination is legitimate while much of it is illegal. Of the various situations in which sex discrimination occurs, the most serious is in employment, education and sports.

While most sex discrimination is directed against women on the job, this is not always the case. Women can perpetrate it against one another. The nurse who resents the young woman physician may be slow to respond to the doctor's orders but quick to respond to the young male physician's requests. Men also have been on the receiving end of sex discrimination.

In one Nova Scotia case, a man responded to a newspaper advertisement for a job as a copywriter with a large retail store. The advertisement indicated that the job was available from May through August and that an ability to type and a Grade 12 education were essential. In applying for the position, the man was told by a woman employment officer that filing an application was a waste of time. She said that the company was looking for a woman to fill the position. Despite the woman's warning, the man submitted an application. He also filed a complaint with the Nova Scotia Human Rights Commission. Following a hearing by a board of inquiry, it was determined that the man was indeed the victim of sex discrimination. The company was instructed to better inform its employees of the store's own nondiscrimination policy and that of the province.

## Employment

How often does an advertisement read "Foreman Wanted," "Waitress Needed," "Workmen-Employment Available?" Even in provinces where such sexual ads are not permitted, how frequently are the job descriptions written so as to make it obvious that despite a neutral title, people of one sex or the other are excluded? Even with the small print caption, "Open to men and women," the sex bias may still be obvious.

Some of the discrimination is done unintentionally, out of habit. In other cases, it is intentional. Restauranteurs may want to hire women only, thinking they can pay them less than men. Others may hire men only, arguing that women on the job would cause slowdowns in production, lower morale, provide a distraction to the men or would be more expensive, as they require separate washroom facilities. Still other employers believe that either the presence of women in heavy industry is unbecoming or that female employees would be incapable of performing heavy work.

With the passage of human rights laws across Canada, the incidence of blatant sex discrimination has decreased, but episodes of more subtle forms of sex discrimination continue to occur. Since women have been long denied entry into certain sectors, they have not had as much experience as their male counterparts. Knowing this, employers who wish to prevent women from going up the job ladder can set years of experience as a criterion. It looks as if experience is job-related, but in fact experience may not be necessary to perform the job properly. Women not having the appropriate number of years experience are denied advancement.

Height and weight requirements which are not on the surface sex-related and which appear to be job-related may in fact be neither.

Human Rights Commissions will look at the real purpose for such criteria in determining whether there has been discrimination.

## Sexual Harrassment

A number of cases of sexual harrassment rather than discrimination have come before human rights commissions throughout Canada. A restaurant owner in Niagara Falls was charged by two waitresses with firing them after they refused his sexual advances. Although the Ontario Human Rights Commission found that there was insufficient evidence to support the women's allegations, it did develop a number of guidelines for future sexual harrassment cases. Despite the fact that these guidelines are applicable only in Ontario, the rules may influence Human Rights Commissions in other provinces.

Any sexual "come-on," which is made a condition of employment or job advancement, would clearly be in violation of the human rights laws. Similarly, sexual advancements that create a negative mental or emotional environment in the work setting are not permitted. The Ontario Commission, however, did set certain limits. Social interaction between employer and employee is permissible. So is talk of sex, as long as the employee neither objects to it nor feels that he or she must have sexual relations with the employer in order to stay employed. What would be clearly improper and illegal are such things as unsolicited touching of the employee's person or other unwanted physical contact; degrading sexual remarks and taunting; repeated or continuous propositions; and social or sexual involvement which is made a condition of remaining employed.

## Education

Sex discrimination in education can be found at almost any level, although it is more likely to occur in universities. Subtle and oftentimes indirect in form, sex bias in education may be hidden by a façade of seemingly legitimate rules.

Scholarships are one cause for concern. Some may have been established long ago by well-intentioned alumni or friends of the university. At that time, few women went to university so that there was little incentive to include women among potential scholarship recipients. In other instances, the university was given money for use in awarding scholarships on the understanding that the school would set its own criteria for selecting worthy students. Sex was not mentioned by the donor, but the university would award the funds to an able young man, worthy of the distinction. There have also been scholarships established solely for young women. Although Human Rights Commissions have usually not been given the power to rectify this, some have been successful in persuading scholarship administrators to change their policies.

Where funds are left with specific instruction that male students should receive the scholarships, little can be done to rectify the sex bias. It was, after all, a legitimate gift made at a time when women did not aspire to an education beyond the high school years. If, however, the funds were left to the university to distribute as it saw fit or to a foundation to decide who should receive funds, it may be quite another matter. When the university or foundation uses criteria which reflect a sex bias unrelated to the donor's intent, it could result in charges of discrimination. Unfortunately, the situation is not covered by the provincial human rights acts, so that apart from the persuasive authority of the Human Rights Commissions, nothing can be done.

Blatant sexual discrimination against women being admitted to certain faculties, or men to nursing schools, seems to be a thing of the past because of human rights laws. What is now possible is that schools may give considerable weight to such factors as sex, without expressly stating so. It may be difficult to prove.

The most trying form of sex discrimination in education occurs not at the hands of administrators or boards, but from fellow students and faculty. Female students are particularly vulnerable to this type of sex bias, though male students in traditionally all-female areas have also suffered from it. Off-color jokes, sexist remarks and insults from professors and classmates are not uncommon. A good grade in return for a sexual "favor" is also found on campuses. Still other female students have been lectured by male professors on how wrong it is for women to be in medical school when they should be getting married and having babies. Female medical students may also face discrimination in being barred from examining male patients. There are still professors who refer to their coeducation classes as "Gentlemen!" The law is powerless in curbing these attitudes which may discourage many would-be students.

Some faculty members have been known to set higher standards for women to meet than for male students. The idea behind these unequal standards is that it will cause a number of women to drop out. Placement officers at schools may arrange better job interviews for men or direct them towards superior jobs. In all these cases, trying to prove sex discrimination is very difficult. It is almost impossible to document, and those overhearing sexist remarks or observing biased practices may be reluctant to come forward. Only a change in attitude will overcome the problem. Recent successes are largely due to this change.

Men have also faced discrimination in faculties and schools for traditionally female occupations, such as nursing. The peer pressure of female classmates and male friends may raise questions about the student's masculinity. The student may also be resented by female classmates who fear that, as in other fields, the man will take the best-paying jobs with the best chance of advancement. At least in an all-female profession, women are protected against discrimination of this sort. The proof of this problem has been in the library science profession which is largely dominated by women. The majority of top jobs in Canadian libraries are held by men.

## Sports

As in many forms of social activities, men and women are often segregated in sports. There are of course exceptions, but the general rule is that men and women do not compete against each other. Teams are made up of either men or women, not both. In the few sports that allow both sexes, men and women must be matched equally, as in mixed doubles in tennis—one man and one woman on each side. This instance has lead to Olympic scandals, with Soviet men allegedly passing themselves off as women in order to compete with women.

Traditionally, most recreational group activities were conducted separately. Sports followed this pattern. Culturally, it was not acceptable for women to play certain sports, such as rugby or North American football, though they could play sports as rough as ground hockey.

It has also been considered indecent to pit men and women against each other in contact sports, since in our society any touching of the opposite sex is considered a sexual act. People of the same sex touching each other in a contact sport is not generally considered sexual and is, therefore, acceptable.

For these reasons, women and men are not often given the opportunity to compete openly with and against anyone else of the opposite sex. These attitudes are so ingrained in society that when one American girl was finally permitted to play on a previously all-boys' baseball team, she was forced to participate in a totally "equal" manner, which included the wearing of a jock strap with protective cupping.

When challenged on their discriminatory practices, sports officials usually give three reasons: 1) extra change rooms and shower facilities would be required at great cost; 2) contact and violent sports with men could result in injuries to female participants; 3) it is unfair to pit women against men, since the women do not have the same strength, agility and endurance. In many cases, these justifications may be correct. If a woman is agreeable, however, to changing clothes in other quarters, or showering before the men come in or after they have left, is the facility objection still a valid ground for barring her from participation? If the sport is neither contact nor violent, is the reason of potential physical injury justified? Even in contact sports, can it always be said that all women are any more vulnerable to injury than men? In many areas, most women generally do not have the same strength, agility and endurance as most men. If, however, an individual woman does have the same strength, agility and endurance as a man, can her exclusion be justified?

In individual cases where these reasons are unfounded, is the fact that men and women have not traditionally played and competed together in most sports a valid reason for continued discrimination? Is it a matter of public decency? In an era when naked men and women display themselves in magazines selling millions of copies and the intimacy of love is shown openly on the screens of neighborhood cinemas, can it be said to affront public decency to have men and women on the same basketball teams? If any individual woman has the ability to compete at the same standard as a man, to deny her the opportunity is clearly discrimination. Whether it falls within the authority of human rights legislation is a matter which requires legal interpretation of the circumstances of each case and of the words of provincial law. Human rights commissions are, however, beginning to move into the sports scene in matters of sex discrimination.

In 1977, a complaint was lodged with the Nova Scotia Human Rights Commission by the father of an 11-year-old girl. The young lady had been denied the opportunity of playing in house league hockey. The father claimed that by excluding his daughter the Yarmouth Minor Hockey Association had violated provisions of the provincial human rights act prohibiting sex discrimination.

A board of inquiry, after hearing all the evidence in the case, found for the female hockey player. The board ordered that the association process the girl's application for registration in the same manner as any other application for registration. The young lady's "victory" was, however, based more on a technicality in the regulations governing minor hockey than an outright, across-the-board ban on sex discrimination in the sport. What is interesting about the board's decision, and perhaps helpful to future challenges of sex discrimination in sports, is that absent are the usual arguments about women in coed sports. Despite this narrow victory for women in hockey, there will be need of more challenges and changes in attitudes among players, parents, coaches and the public before sex discrimination in all sports is resolved.

## Housing

Discrimination in this area, as well as in employment, has traditionally been the greatest barrier to Blacks, Jews and other minorities. While these groups have to a large extent been able to overcome these difficulties, housing discrimination on the basis of sex is still very much a problem. The discrimination often takes the form of discrimination based on marital status. A landlord may refuse to rent an apartment to a single woman or a bachelor due to preconceived notions of wild parties, promiscuity and damage rather than being concerned with the reputation of the individual applicant.

A British Columbia case illustrates the problem. A woman separated from her husband and living with her three children and her mother made an inquiry about a house for rent in Vancouver. The house had a large yard which required considerable gardening. The agent who showed her the house told her that the owners were looking for a family to whom they could rent the house. He also asked the woman if she thought she could handle the property and the rental of $350 per month. She replied that she thought she could. When she learned a few days later that the house had been rented to another party, she filed a complaint with the British Columbia Human Rights Commission.

The Commission determined that the owners feared a single woman could not maintain the house and her family. In ruling that this was a case of unlawful sex discrimination, it was pointed out that the owners had made their decision on the basis of a generalization regarding women separated from their husbands. They had not made an assessment of this particular woman's individual capacity. This form of discrimination based on sex and marital status was said to be inexcusable. The property owners were fined a nominal sum.

## Affirmative Action

Long-standing patterns of sex bias can be redressed under human rights laws by implementing a program of inverse sex discrimination called "affirmative action." Administered under the watchful eye of human rights commissions throughout Canada, affirmative action programs have evolved, by which preferential treatment is given to people of one sex over the other, in order to redress long-standing imbalances.

For example, in order to alleviate the disproportionate number of women in nursing and recognizing the need for male nurses, schools may adopt a policy of preferential admission of men. This would be done for as long as is necessary to correct the imbalance and in accordance with established guidelines. If it is not done under careful supervision, there could be serious charges of government-sponsored sex discrimination.

## Why Sex Discrimination?

As seen throughout this chapter, sex discrimination does not have one single cause. There are many considerations which lead to its existence. Partly, it is sheer ignorance and superstition, or long-standing traditions to treat women or men in a particular way without considering their individual capacities. Many of the policies favoring sex discrimination are based on economic and political factors in which a largely male-dominated society bars women from gaining financial self-sufficiency. Some fear being "shown up" by a member of the opposite sex. It may be an affront to a man's self-esteem to take orders from a woman. In some cases, women feel the same way about other women. The policies which have forged today's sex biases cross all social and economic levels so that one can find wealthy and poor alike sharing the same outlook. The law, as a reflection of society, has consciously or unconsciously reinforced many of these attitudes. As society changes, the law follows, with changes in legislation, changes in court decisions and changes in the administration of law. It is, however, a slow and often frustrating process for those who want immediate reforms.

Human Rights Commissions throughout Canada have done a credible job in eliminating sex discrimination. Human rights as a whole, and in particular sexual inequality, will continue to be a standard around which people will rally for years to come. As more people question discrimination based on sex, more changes will occur. Much of the reform will not come from law. It will come about slowly through changes in social attitudes and customs. It promises to be a long process.

# 11 The Law Through "Gay" Eyes

Until recently, the homosexual and lesbian communities existed behind a cloud of darkness. Few openly admitted their sexual preference for persons of the same sex. Social pressures, including threats of physical harm, blackmail and loss of jobs, pressured gay people into hiding their true feelings. Few laws, if any, existed to protect them.

In recent years, gay people have emerged as a vocal and somewhat politically active force. In seeking to overcome what they see as years of social injustice, to clarify and establish legal rights, gays have encountered many stumbling blocks. Many of the problems have involved marriage, divorce, custody and adoption. These issues have formed the basis for attempts at legislative reform. Change in these areas has not come easily, and many people question whether social and legal reforms are even necessary. If gays constitute only ten percent of Canadian society, one may well ask, "why bother?"

## Marriage Between Persons of the Same Sex

Marriage has been broadly defined throughout the centuries as the union for life of two persons of the opposite sex. Marriage is a contract with mutual rights and obligations. Yet marriage is more than the usual contract. It gives each partner a legal status: "husband and wife." In this contract and special status, sex is a key determinant of the relationship between man and woman, since from it comes the continuation of the human race. Society naturally expects that if a man and woman marry—barring reproductive difficulties—they will have a family. The law, building upon society's expectation, through court decisions and statutes, has reinforced this notion of heterosexual marriage. The question is: how do homosexual marriages fit into this framework? The answer is they do not. They are not legally possible.

In 1974, two men went through a marriage ceremony in Manitoba with the intention of becoming a married couple. All the appropriate papers were completed and the requirements of the law regulating marriage ceremonies were followed. When they attempted to register their marriage, the Registrar refused to do so. In his administrative discretion, he was not satisfied as to the truth and sufficiency of the marriage. Upset with the Registrar's decision, the couple asked a court to force the official to register their marriage. Although the court recognized that the couple had met the requirements of the marriage law, and nothing in the laws of Manitoba or Canada specifically prevented the marriage of two men, the court determined that the Registrar was within his rights to refuse to recognize the "marriage" as a legal marriage. In declining the couple's request, the court relied upon the Common Law idea that marriage is a mainspring of family life and the continued existence of humanity. Since future generations can only result from heterosexual relationships, a "marriage" between two persons of the same sex is legally invalid.

The attitude throughout Canada, the United States and the United Kingdom is the same. In the eyes of the law persons of the same sex cannot marry each other. On this basis, homosexual and lesbian couples have been denied marriage licenses. Yet one English court seems to have recognized a "gay marriage" in order to dissolve it.

Prior to the marriage, the wife had undergone a sex change operation. The husband knew that his wife had been born a male. Shortly after their marriage, however, the husband sought to nullify the marriage on the grounds that his wife was a male. The court agreed. Despite the surgical removal of his scrotum and penis, the creation of an artificial vagina and female breast development, the wife was really a male. Since English law only recognizes the validity of heterosexual unions, the marriage was null and void.

No court has recognized the validity of a gay marriage, nor are there any statutes which would give it legal status. The marriage laws are based upon society's long-standing attitudes towards marriage. Since the law changes in response to modifications in societal norms, it is likely that one day the laws regulating gay marriages will change as well.

## Divorce and the Gay Spouse

Under the Canadian Divorce Act, a spouse can seek a divorce based on the allegation that since his or her marriage the other partner has engaged in a homosexual act. The law does not define what is meant by a homosexual act. At least two court decisions, however, have interpreted the legal meaning of this phrase.

In one case from Prince Edward Island, a husband on several occasions found his wife and another woman naked in bed hugging and kissing to the point of mutual orgasm. He filed for divorce under the homosexuality provision and the court granted the divorce decree. The court indicated that the sexual activity seen by the husband between his wife and lesbian lover constituted homosexual activity.

In another case from Saskatchewan, a divorce was also granted on the ground of homosexual activity by the wife. During testimony in court, the wife admitted that she and her female lover had caressed each other's breasts. The court noted that caressing the breasts in a heterosexual relationship was certainly sexual. The same would be true in a homosexual liaison. There was no proof of sexual gratification, as in the Prince Edward Island case, but the Saskatchewan court said none was necessary. Episodes of hugging, kissing and the like were sufficient proof of homosexual activity.

It would seem that in Canada a divorce will be granted on the basis of sufficient evidence of homosexual activity on the part of the other spouse. The evidence required includes eyewitness testimony of homosexual exchanges or an admission by the spouse that he or she is involved in a homosexual affair.

## Custody and the Homosexual Parent

Traditionally, when a couple separated and divorced, society expected that the wife would take custody of any children of that marriage. It was felt that the mother could provide the stable home life which is particularly important for young children. This notion of custody going to the mother was also reinforced by the fact that few mothers worked, and if they did, it was only on a part-time basis. Since the mother was home anyway, she should get control of the children, or so the line of reasoning went.

The law reflected the general idea of one-sided custody. It did so by invoking a long-standing legal principle that whatever is done that directly affects a child, the decision must be in his or her "best interests." What may be in the best interests of one child may not be so in the case of another. It is largely decided on a case-by-case basis. In custody matters, the law followed society's expectations and most of the time awarded custody of the child to the mother. Judges felt that a working father was ill-equipped to support and care for youngsters, pay alimony to his wife and hire a housekeeper.

Both society and law have changed. More women take an active role in the work force. Fathers are spending more time with their children. In some instances, wives are supporting their husbands and children. With the changing role of women has come a rethinking of what is in the child's best interests in a custody dispute. It is now not uncommon to see a father awarded custody of his children. It has involved a more thorough review of the circumstances in each case.

Particular concerns arise when the divorce involves the revelation that one of the spouses is gay. Should the gay parent receive custody of his or her child? Will they push their child into a gay life style? Will it cause the child ridicule and embarrassment in the eyes of his peers? Is it in the best interests of the child to live with the gay parent and his or her gay friend?

In Canada, the subject has received a considerable amount of attention in the courts. In one case from Saskatchewan, the mother, a professed lesbian, was denied custody of her children. The judge explained that the lack of testimony from the woman with whom the mother was living was a serious flaw in her case. Without hearing more about this woman and her character, the judge felt that he had an insufficient basis upon which to assess her possible influence on the children. This factor, in addition to the father being strong, firm and generous with his children, led to his receiving custody of the children. The court treated the case much like a woman living with her male lover. It was clearly stated that homosexuality is not in itself a basis for denying a parent his or her right to custody. However, in this situation the court feared that this particular mother's life style would put the children in touch with persons of abnormal taste and tendencies.

A few years later a court in Alberta reached the opposite conclusion in another case of a lesbian seeking custody of her children. In that situation, the woman with whom the mother was living gave evidence to the judge which reassured him that she would not be a detrimental influence on the children. Unlike the earlier Saskatchewan case, this mother did not flaunt her homosexuality in public nor did she view it as a mission to convert others to her life style. She was a far better parent than the father, who was habitually on drugs.

Judging from these cases, it appears that there are two major factors a court will assess in deciding what is in a child's best interests in a custody battle involving a gay parent: 1) those factors in the situation which make it possible that the child will become a homosexual; 2) the community's reaction being so negative and severe that it will cause the child serious harm. Apart from these concerns, the fact that a parent is gay is not enough for a court to deny him or her custody of the child.

## Adoption

In adoptions involving gay parents, many of the factors considered in custody disputes apply. The questions raised, however, may be different. Does the fact that a person is gay bar them from adopting a child? May a court preclude a lesbian from adopting a girl and a male homosexual a boy? Some of these questions have not been addressed by courts or provincial assemblies, but in some situations one can speculate likely responses on the basis of similar matters.

Unlike custody, in adoption the natural or biological parents give up all rights and obligations towards the child including the right to visit their child. Since the court's decision is permanent, it is important that the judge knows the feelings of both biological parents. The court must weigh the needs of the child and, looking at the situation as broadly as possible, decide what is in the youngster's best interests, what best serves his welfare. While the court must consider the rights of the parents, it is the child's interest that takes priority. It is, however, as one judge phrased it an "emotional guillotine" to remove all rights from the parent toward the child.

In one English case, a child's parents separated and divorced when he was about a year old. His mother was granted a divorce on the basis that her husband's homosexuality amounted to cruelty. She subsequently remarried and she and her new husband attempted to adopt the infant. This would have effectively stopped all contact between the boy and his father. A judge ruled that the mother and her second husband could proceed without first gaining the gay parent's consent to the adoption. To the judge, given the father's homosexuality, his constant refusal to allow the adoption was unreasonable. The father successfully appealed the case. The appeal court stated that the father's refusal to consent was quite reasonable, given the lasting and permanent nature of adoption. That the father was a homosexual was not as important as how he handled his homosexuality. Were he to turn his homosexuality into a crusade of sorts, and attempt to convert his son to a gay life-style, the court would not have acted in favor of the father. In this case, the father assured the judge that during the boy's impressionable years he would visit with him at his paternal grandparent's home. In this setting, adequate safeguards could be followed to limit any harm stemming from the father's homosexuality.

Homosexuality and adoption taken separately are highly emotional problems. When brought together as factors in a single case, the atmosphere becomes tense, confused and difficult. Courts are asked to make far-reaching decisions as to who gets permanent rights to a child based on his welfare and best interests. In some cases, adoption by the "straight" parent would be far better, but in other situations it is best to allow the gay parent to adopt his or her child. The difficulty, as in all aspects of law, is to decide what is best for the child, the parents and society, in each case. It is a matter of law reflecting society. As society changes, so too will the law.

## Homosexuality and Employment

Gays face a serious problem in employment. Some are hired and carry out their tasks in a fine manner, only to be fired when their employer learns they are gay. Others are denied jobs at the outset, the prospective employer believing them to be a potentially bad or disruptive influence upon their fellow workers.

Should homosexuals be denied certain jobs? Is this sex discrimination and if it is, should it be allowed? Should a gay man or woman be denied a teaching post at an elementary school or high school? If a person does not flaunt his gay life style or try to influence others, should his homosexuality even be considered by an employer?

Some of these issues are difficult to address since the employer can deny the homosexual a job and base his decision on what appear to be perfectly reasonable, nonsexual factors. In these cases, the homosexuality issue is a real, but hidden, issue. From time to time, however, there are confrontations clearly based on homosexuality.

John Damien was a race track steward with the Ontario Racing Commission. Having worked much of his life in caring for and training horses, he had worked his way up to a comfortable $25,000 per year job. John Damien was gay. He kept his homosexuality to himself. He never flaunted it in public or at work. In 1975, he was fired for being morally unsuitable for his post. A doctor retained by the racing authority who had once treated Damien had leaked confidential medical information to race authorities. Damien soon learned that word had spread throughout Canada and he was unable to find employment in his field. Without adequate employment and high legal fees from a lawsuit challenging his former employers, Damien went bankrupt. His lawsuit against his former employer never reached the Ontario courts.

Some would think Damien should have sought help from the Ontario Human Rights Commission. Damien did, only to find out that Ontario human rights legislation does not extend to job security for homosexuals. Only Quebec has laws banning discrimination against gays in employment.

Gay teachers, particularly those in elementary and high schools, pose another issue. If a teacher is overtly gay and tries to convince his or her students to follow a homosexual life-style, it would likely be sufficient basis for firing him or not renewing his contract. It is argued, however, that the teacher who is gay in his private life and does not try to influence his pupils should not be dismissed. Others respond that the privately gay teacher who is known to be a homosexual may provide a detrimental role model for impressionable youngsters. Lost in the controversy is the fact that many heterosexual teachers, and in fact many youth leaders, may themselves provide detrimental examples because of their private but known activities.

Without laws specifically recognizing the rights of heterosexuals and homosexuals in the job setting, more Damien cases will likely occur. Society and the law have not found the right formula for accommodating the rights of gays and straights. This is a sensitive issue and it may take quite awhile to reach a workable response.

## Human Rights for Homosexuals

Most provincial human rights laws ban sexual discrimination in such matters as employment, holding property, housing and public services. Only the Quebec Charter of Human Rights and Freedoms is interpreted to include homosexuality under the ban against sex discrimination. No other province specifically prohibits discrimination on the basis of homosexuality or sexual preference.

There have been some tests of the Quebec law. In Rimouski, for example, two Montreal men who had been dancing together were thrown off a dance floor at a local discotheque. A complaint was filed with the Quebec Human Rights Commission which determined that the nightclub had acted improperly. The club was ordered to apologize to the men and to pay each man $100 in damages.

In another case, the Association pour les droits de la communauté gaie du Québec (ADGA), a gay rights group, charged the Montreal Catholic School Commission with unlawful sex discrimination in denying them rental space for one evening in one of the Commission's schools. The Quebec Human Rights Commission determined that the School Commission had not violated the law, pointing to an exception in the law which permits discrimination by philanthropic, religious and educational organizations. The issue was taken to court where it was decided that the Catholic School Commission had indeed violated the Human Rights Charter. The court stated that any exception to the human rights law had to be interpreted quite narrowly. There had been no objective justification for the School Commission's actions in denying rental space to the gay group.

Ontario is among a number of provinces that are currently considering major revisions of their human rights laws. With the growing political activism in the gay community and increased interest in gay rights, provisions will likely be added to ban discrimination on the basis of sexual preference in a number of provinces.

## What's Next for Gay Rights?

Increased awareness of homosexuality and gay rights will undoubtedly lead to a variety of legal confrontations. Challenges to existing laws and accepted social mores are bound to occur. Housing and employment for gays will certainly be key issues, as well as the legal recognition of gay marriages. The issuance of passports to gays, the practices of the military service, and discrimination in the securing of loans will likely generate legislative review or court action. Virtually every aspect of daily life that "straight" people take for granted will probably form the basis for a gay rights problem and eventual solution. Until answers are found, however, society must wrestle with its response to the demand for recognition of gay rights.

# 12 Sex Change

## What is it? Is it Legal?

A woman trapped in a man's body. Or a man trapped in a woman's body. This is how thousands of people seeking sex reassignment operations describe themselves. They tell their psychiatrists they have all the feelings, the desires of a woman, but are burdened by the body of a man. They resent their deep voices, their beards, their sexual organs. They dress as women, but know they are still men. They are not transvestites, men who get a thrill out of dressing in women's clothing. They are not homosexuals, since they feel attracted to men in the way women are attracted to men, not in the way homosexual men are attracted to other men. They have none of the physical sex characteristics of women. They are physically, totally male. Society treats them accordingly, and they hate it. In their own eyes they are women. Similarly, there are women who feel that they are men.

The frustration and torment is unending. It has led to self-mutilation and to suicide. It has led to years of psychiatric treatment, often without success. There is often no way of changing the mind to suit the body.

If the mind cannot be changed to suit the body, why not the body to fit the mind? If American Christine Jorgenson could do it and British author Jan (nee James) Morris, why not everyone who wants to change their sex? During the last few decades, the highly publicized

Scandinavian operations were made available in many hospitals in the United States and Canada. Months of preparatory psychotherapy and psychological testing are required. Social adjustments of living as a member of the opposite sex, dressing like them and using the public washrooms of the other sex are part of the "treatment." Hormone treatment is used to minimize the existing physical characteristics and to create breasts. The climax is surgery—castration of the testes, amputation of the penis and the creation of an artificial vagina. Menstruation and child bearing are not possible, but sexual intercourse is. The result is an individual who looks like a woman, both dressed and undressed, speaks like a woman, acts like a woman, feels like a woman and is treated like a woman. The question: Is she a woman?

In a smaller number of cases women have become men. By the artistry of the plastic surgeon breasts are removed, the vagina is closed and a penis created. There have even been claims suggesting that intercourse, to a limited extent, has been possible. Fertility is, of course, not possible. "He-men" they may not be, but are they men?

## Sex Change and The Law

The first underlying question that must be asked is: Are sex change operations legal? The Criminal Code of Canada is silent on the matter. It does, however, specifically protect everyone "from criminal responsibility for performing a surgical operation" for the benefit of the patient if the operation is performed with reasonable care and skill and if it is reasonable to perform the operation. It would be very difficult to prove that a sex change operation involving a number of medical consultants did not fit these criteria.

A further question is whether the operation is illegal for being repugnant to public policy. If this were true, it would mean that a patient would not be able to request it. While this has not been tested in Canadian courts, such a finding is unlikely. For the judges to tell the medical profession that a particular operation for the benefit of the patient, however risky, is against public policy is difficult to imagine. It is particularly difficult to imagine since sex reassignment surgery is only employed when all other methods of treatment, such as psychotherapy, have failed.

## Who Pays?

In Canada, patients often assume that hospital and medical care are free. This is an understandable view since most provinces do not charge premiums. What patients forget is that while most of the funding comes from taxes (even where there are premiums), the programs are still like insurance plans. There are limits on the services that are insured. The basic requirement for any medical or hospital service to be insured by the provincial health insurance plans is that it be medically necessary.

As long as surgery is considered by the health insurance authorities to be medically necessary, it will be insured. If, however, the insurance authorities do not think so, it will not be insured and the patient will bear the thousands of dollars in costs. The insurance authorities may regard it as experimental, or the chance of its success so low as not to be "medically necessary."

Depending on the province, the patient must be aware of the different requirements for receiving medical or hospital treatment outside his or her own province, or outside Canada. Some provinces will only pay for care that cannot medically be provided within its borders. This limits out-of-province coverage to emergencies and care that is referred by a local physician on the basis that such service cannot be provided within the province. There are also limits on the amount that will be paid, especially outside Canada. Each province has a different policy which may vary from time to time. The attitude, therefore, of provincial health insurance authorities can seriously affect whether a person can go through with sex reassignment. This is particularly true in the case of provinces where this type of treatment is not available.

## The Legal Effects

Regardless of how successful sex change operations may be, and many have been disasters, the primary question which continues to arise is: Has the person really changed their sex? While many of the physical attributes are similar to those of their adopted sex, they have not adopted all the attributes. Their bone structure remains that of their original sex. The chromosomes found in the cells of the body retain the characteristics of the original sex. There may be other characteristics that remain the same.

No statute of the federal or of any provincial legislature has defined what it means to be male or female. Yet the legal effect of being male or female is important to one's position in society. The law treats men and women differently. They have different rights and duties. It is vital, therefore, to know whether a person is of one or the other sex.

We also describe people not by their names but by their sexual designation or by a designation implying their sex. Certain legal rights or duties may be given to a brother, but not a sister; a mother, but not a father.

There are five major legal problems arising from a sex change operation. Some have been settled by legislation, some by the courts and others remain unsolved. Each must be examined in turn.

## Problem One: Change of Name

The first practical problem facing the individual who has undergone sex change is that of changing his or her name. All Canadian provinces and the two territories have legislation allowing a person to change their name and setting out a procedure for it. The change may take place either before or after the operation, except in Quebec, where the Change of Name Act specifically states that it can only take place after the person has "successfully undergone medical treatments." The change of name in Quebec is also restricted to unmarried persons. In other provinces, as a matter of practice, the application for a change of name would also take place after the change of sex has been accomplished.

## Problem Two: Change of Birth Certificate

One of the most important documents required in our bureaucratic society is the birth certificate. Its popularity may have given way to the driver's license and the social insurance card, but it is still the most accurate identity document. Licenses can go out of date. Social insurance cards can be duplicated. The traditional birth certificate was meant to be forever.

The place of birth and the date never change. The sex of the person cannot change either, since it signifies the sex at the time of birth. For someone having undergone sex change, the card is still accurate since it reflects facts at birth, not those presently in existence. What then is the problem? How can a birth certificate be changed to describe a condition which was not in evidence at the time of birth?

All provinces allow changes to be made in birth registration upon which the certificate is based if the registration was based on incorrect information. In some cases, a baby has been designated one gender when in fact it is the other. Until recently, logic prevailed and the sex-changed person was saddled with a document identifying him as a member of his or her previous sex. As a result of this identification, the person would not be treated according to his or her "new" sex but according to the previous sex.

The embarrassment and the legal consequences are severe. It could affect the person's ability to obtain other documents such as passports, to get insurance, or to assert any rights requiring identification by birth certificate.

To overcome these hardships, most provinces have amended their legislation to allow for changes in the birth certificate. A procedure is established in which medical certificates are presented to the registrar of births. In most provinces, the change can be made by any "person who has undergone transsexual surgery" (Saskatchewan) or "has had his anatomical sex structure changed to a sex other than that which appears on his registration of birth" (Ontario, Nova Scotia). Other provinces, however, such as New Brunswick and British Columbia, only allow unmarried people to make an application. The implication is: Get divorced first!

Some provinces were somewhat concerned with the problem of whether the sex could really be changed. For this reason, many of the laws refer to "anatomical sex," implying that there is another sort which is not changed. Scientifically, this is quite correct.

British Columbia was concerned that the results of a sex change operation really did not change the sex. To overcome these worries, that province allows the new registration to be "consistent with the intended result of the transsexual surgery." Saskatchewan was not about to guess. They allow a new registration if the sex has really been changed, "so that the designation will be consistent with the results."

## Problem Three: Change of Passport

Since a passport identifies a person as they presently appear, not as the way they once were, there are no legal impediments to changing any sex designation that may be stated. The difficulty is simply to convince the passport officials that the person applying for the new passport is the same as the holder of the previous one. This can be done by documentary evidence that the person's sex has been changed. A medical certificate, preferably a sworn statement, by a doctor that the person has a new sex but is the same person should be satisfactory.

## Problem Four: Is Sex Change a Defense to a Crime?

There are many crimes under the Criminal Code of Canada which can only be committed against women. A man cannot be raped by another man. He can only be indecently assaulted. It is a criminal offense to knowingly conceal a woman in a "common bawdy-house," but not a man. It is also an offense to give a woman "any drug, intoxicating liquor, matter, or thing with intent to stupify or overpower her in order thereby to enable any person to have illicit sexual intercourse with her." The innocent virgin male is left defenseless by the Criminal Code against the drug-laden liberated Amazon.

Is it a defense for the accused to say there was no rape, since the ravished young lady was actually a young man? The accused did intend to rape a young lady. Is that enough to convict him? So far Canadian courts have not been faced with this dilemma. Since rape is a crime which requires the penetration by the accused into the vagina of the victim, and that penetration took place into what certainly appears to be the vagina of a female, it would be surprising indeed to say that the victim was a male.

In each of these cases, the courts would examine the words used in the Code to determine who Parliament was trying to protect and what type of conduct it was trying to stop. Since the conduct against an ordinary member of the weaker sex is the same as against someone who has all of its attributes for the purpose of fulfilling the conduct prohibited, defense of sex change would be difficult to prove.

## Problem Five: Marriage

John loves Mary. John marries Mary. John and Mary seal their union in matrimonial consummation. And then, surprise to John, he finds out his wife, Mary, used to be Martin. What does this do to the marriage? Is John married to another man? Is it grounds for divorce? Was it ever a marriage at all?

Suppose, on the other hand, that John and Mary are married. Both are biologically correct members of the opposite sex and always have been. They have two children. John, however, is unhappy. He feels that he is a woman trapped in the body of a man. He undergoes sex reassignment and becomes Jennifer. What is the legal effect on that marriage? Is it grounds for divorce? If Mary agreed to John becoming Jennifer and wants to remain married, can she? Is it still a valid marriage?

The crux of the problem is the definition of marriage. In 1866, Sir J. P. Wilde (later Lord Penzance) in the English case of *Hyde* v. *Hyde and Woodmansee* defined it as "...the voluntary union for life of one man and one woman to the exclusion of all others." People of the same sex cannot be married. In 1975, a Manitoba county court would not recognize a "marriage" ceremony between two men, in the case of *North* v. *Matheson.*

In a 1976 New Jersey case of *M. T.* v. *J. T.* a man who had become a woman was considered to be a woman for marriage purposes. In the 1974 New York case of *Frances B.* v. *Mark B.,* however, a woman who changed her sex, but lacked functional genitalia, was regarded by the court as female. It would appear from these court decisions that a legally valid marriage can only exist between a man and a woman.

The controversial 1970 English case of *Corbett* v. *Corbett* presents a situation akin to that of John and Mary (nee Martin). In this case, the court was asked to examine the marriage of a man and a woman who had previously been a man. Mr. Justice Ormrod said that there are five criteria for determining one's sex: 1) chromosomal factors (female XX, male XY); 2) gonadal factors (i.e. presence or absence of testes or ovaries); 3) genital factors (including internal sex organs); 4) psychological factors; and 5) hormonal factors and secondary sex characteristics (e.g. distribution of body hair, breast development, physique). The judge determined the sex of the wife in question on the basis of the first three, at least for the purpose of marriage. The result was that regardless of any surgery, the wife was still a man and therefore the marriage was void and invalid.

This case raises the very interesting question in Canada of whether the change in birth certificate would allow a person to marry in the role of the new sex. While the question has never come before the courts, the answer may be in the negative. The change in the birth certificate allows for better identification of the individual. It does not change the fact that for the purpose of marriage, the newborn woman still may be considered a man. A marriage, therefore, with another man is out of the question.

If John and Mary ended up in a Canadian court with John seeking an annulment, that is, a declaration that he and Mary were never legally married, he would probably get it. It also means that Mary, who for purposes of marriage is still regarded as a man, cannot, for obvious physical reasons, marry a woman either.

The second case of John becoming Jennifer is much more difficult. The original marriage is clearly valid. John and Mary were clearly one man and one woman entering into matrimony. If Mary were opposed to her husband becoming a woman, it would not be difficult for a court to grant her a divorce on the basis of cruelty. If, however, she did not oppose it, the question ordinarily would not arise, since Jennifer and Mary would continue to live together with their children. The question might arise if Mary, while enjoying the benefits of Jennifer's society, missed out on the intimate benefits of marriage, and she sought them elsewhere. Then Jennifer could sue for divorce on grounds of adultery, but Mary's extramarital activities would be adulterous only if she and Jennifer were actually married. Since the marriage was originally between a man and a woman, it would have to be considered valid.

The courts have not been faced with this challenge, but given their attitude in the past, it is difficult to see how such a marriage could remain legally intact. If the logic of Mr. Justice Ormrod in the case of *Corbett* v. *Corbett* were to be applied to this fictional case of *Mary* v. *Jennifer,* Jennifer would be considered a male married to a female. In addition, all criteria required for a valid marriage would have been fulfilled. A male has married a female and the union has been consummated. This would mean that the marriage was valid even after John became Jennifer and Mary has committed adultery. Therefore the divorce must be granted. It remains to be seen if the ingenuity of the courts will solve the puzzle.

## Problem Six: Claims for Benefits

Many wills, insurance policies and sometimes contracts are written in such a way as to give certain benefits to people who are designated not by their name but by their sex. Clauses in wills leaving money to my eldest brother's eldest son are fairly common. What happens if the brother becomes a sister? And the eldest son a daughter? The eldest son of the second eldest brother now wants the money since his father is now the eldest.

These problems can be avoided by specifically naming people, but this is not always possible. The eldest son may not yet be born. The court would examine, in each case, the words of the document in an attempt to determine what the writer really intended. Did he intend to give the money or the property to a particular individual or to a person who is in a particular position? The court will also look at what the facts were at the time of death—not at the time the will, if it is a will, was written.

As in the marriage situation, the courts will be faced with the problem of whether the Jennifer who is a daughter for birth certificate purposes may be a son for purposes of claiming under a will. So far there are no definite legal answers.

## Problem Seven: Discrimination

The chapter on human rights clearly indicates that all provinces and the federal Parliament have passed human rights acts prohibiting discrimination on the basis of sex. No one may be refused employment, housing or access to services solely on the basis of their sex, that is male or female, except in narrowly defined circumstances.

There may be circumstances in which a landlord will not rent to, or an employer hire, a person who has undergone sex reassignment. They will rent to or hire a person who has always been male or female but not one who has changed. None of the human rights acts specifically refer to such a situation. The only way to prevent such discrimination would be for a Human Rights Commission or the court to interpret sex so broadly as to include sex change. The other alternative would be to interpret the prohibition against discrimination of the physically handicapped as including the sexually changed person. Until cases of this nature are fought out in the commissions and courts of Canada, the matter will still be an unanswered question.

Canadian Press carried a report from Toronto in June 1980 about a man who underwent a sex change operation and applied to become an Anglican nun at the St. John's Convent. The dean of the diocese, in reporting on the situation, said that the mother superior felt she had enough problems without taking that on. This undoubtedly sums it up.

# 13 Exhibitionism, Indecent Exposure and Peeping Toms

A woman in Saskatoon stands at her kitchen sink looking out her window. Spring has come in all its peace and beauty to Saskatchewan. The sun is shining, the flowers are budding and the birds are chirping. Suddenly the serenity of the day is shattered. Standing in her garden facing her is a well-dressed young man, his fly unzipped, showing her his penis.

Another woman walking down a street in Rimouski at twilight notices a man urinating against a building. A drunken man stumbles along by a Toronto schoolyard as children race past him on their way home. Only some of the children notice that the man's pants are torn and his genitials are exposed.

Do each of these episodes involve exhibitionism? Can these men be charged with violating the Criminal Code of Canada? Would the situation be any different if it occurred on a public beach and the source of disruption was a beautiful young woman lying facedown on the sand? Is exhibitionism a signal that the person is mentally ill or dangerous? Do exhibitionists usually go on to become rapists?

Over the years, Canadian courts have been faced with various types of cases labelled by the law enforcement officers as "exhibitionism." Some of these cases have ended in acquittal, since Crown prosecutors and police have difficulty in matching exhibitionist behavior to the requirements of the Criminal Code. In some instances the criminal law has been found not to apply at all.

As the law has wrestled with exhibitionism, so too has medicine. Psychiatrists and clinical psychologists have developed certain standards for what characterizes the typical exhibitionist. There have been attempts at psychiatric treatment, including behavior modification. Some of them have worked, but many attempts at a cure have resulted in failure.

A different type of behavior which causes many people to become terribly upset is that of the "Peeping Tom." This is the activity of lurking outside private homes and peering inside in the hope of catching a glimpse of the inhabitants in the nude, in their underwear or as they are dressing or undressing. "Peeping Toms" have been around for centuries. The question is: Can they be punished under the criminal law?

## What is Exhibitionism? The Legal Perspective

There are two sections of the Criminal Code that have been applied to cases of exhibitionism. Section 169 makes it a crime to willfully do an indecent act in a public place in the presence of one or more persons. It also punishes those who willfully do an indecent act in any place with the intent to offend or insult another person. "Indecent act" is not defined, but it should not be confused with gross indecency. (See Chapter Two, *Sex How and With Whom.*)

Section 170 of the Criminal Code deals with nudity. It makes it a crime to appear in the nude in a public place or on private property with a public view. It does not matter whether the property is owned by the individual. Section 170 applies unless the person had a lawful excuse to appear in the nude. As defined in this portion of the Criminal Code, "nude" refers to anyone who "is so clad as to offend against public decency or order." In other words, the accused does not have to be naked to be nude. Unlike section 169, in prosecutions under the nudity section a case cannot be undertaken without the consent of the provincial attorney general.

The discretion given provincial attorneys general under section 170 is twofold. The federal Parliament recognized that not all cases of public nudity require criminal sanctions in order to maintain peace and order. The decision to prosecute, it is believed, is best left to each provincial attorney general. Parliament apparently recognized that what may be disruptive in Saint John, New Brunswick, may not be in Vancouver.

The other consideration is that the discretion given to each attorney general acts as a safeguard against criminal prosecutions requested by overly sensitive citizens. To some people, the slightest suggestion of nudity is enough for them to demand criminal prosecutions. For the overwhelming majority, the situation probably falls well within the norms of moral decency.

In applying sections 169 and 170 of the Criminal Code, the courts have been faced with a variety of cases involving various stages of nudity. Successful prosecutions under section 169 require proof that the nude or partially clothed person acted in a shameful manner or in extremely poor taste. Nudity alone is not enough for a conviction under this part of the Criminal Code. Section 170, however, would appear to punish nudity or partial nudity which offends public decency. It more or less sets standards of dress rather than punishes particular acts which society might find shameful or unseemly. The application of and differences in interpretation of these sections of the Criminal Code have been well illustrated in a number of interesting cases.

A Saskatchewan man was seen exposing himself in front of a seven-year-old boy. This child had been playing in his front yard with his sister. At one point the man grabbed the boy's arm and pulled the child's hand towards his exposed genitals. The child's mother raced outside and frightened the man away. He was acquitted at trial on the basis that the youngster did not "see" the indecent act. The case was successfully appealed by the Crown prosecutor. The judge said that it was enough that the mother viewed the man's indecent behavior. Given the man's intent and his behavior, there was enough evidence for a conviction under section 169 of the Criminal Code.

In 1977, an Ontario man was charged under section 169 with indecency. The man had been standing in a department store aisle. A female customer was standing not too far away. A woman security officer located on an elevated surveillance platform spotted the man with his genitals exposed, masturbating. She notified other employees who also watched him from secluded locations. As the other store patron moved up the aisle, the man stopped masturbating. After she moved on, however, he resumed his activity. He was charged with violating section 169 and convicted.

The court said that the department store was a public place since the public was invited to enter to shop. The judge said that since the man knew that another customer was nearby and had the opportunity to see him masturbating, the requirements for a conviction had been met. Despite this, the judge dismissed the case. He noted that the man had a wife and two children who depended on him for support. This was the man's first offense. Although the behavior was punishable as a crime, it was more properly categorized as a nuisance. For these reasons the man was set free.

In an earlier case, a British Columbia woman had been charged with violating section 169 of the Code for sunbathing in the nude. The young woman was found by policemen on a beach near the University of British Columbia, lying on her stomach, reading. She was completely naked. Although there were no others around, it was a public beach. Since the incident occurred in August, it was conceivable that others might have been in the area. She was ordered to put on some clothes, arrested and convicted of performing an indecent act in a public place under section 169.

The Supreme Court of British Columbia overturned her conviction. The court said that sunbathing in the nude is not an indecent act as defined in section 169. There was no evidence of what is called moral turpitude or of trying to attract attention to herself. One wonders if the police were forced to charge the young woman under section 169 because the British Columbia Attorney General declined to authorize prosecution under section 170 of her Godiva-like behavior.

Prosecutions under section 170 of the Criminal Code for being nude in a public place are a different matter. Although the facts of the cases brought under section 170 (the "nude" section) are quite similar to prosecutions under section 169 (the "indecent" section), the courts have drawn some distinctions in their interpretation of the Criminal Code.

In July 1975, three young men went skinny-dipping in the South Saskatchewan River not far from Saskatoon. As they stood completely nude on a sand bar, some other people came along to swim at the same location. The three were charged in *R.* v. *Benolkin* with being nude in a public place without a lawful excuse and convicted. Each was fined $200.

The three successfully appealed their convictions. The court felt that section 170 was not intended to punish nude swimming or nudity on a remote shore. The judge said: "It cannot be an offense to swim in the nude at a lonely place in Canada in the summer. That is part of the pleasure of summer in Canada, particularly for young males." It is not a crime, the Saskatchewan court said, to misjudge the loneliness of a place for skinny-dipping. The three had a lawful excuse for their nudity in that their behavior was not disorderly, immoral or indecent.

The Supreme Court of Canada took quite a different position in another case brought under section 170. In *R. v. Verrette*, a young man had been charged and convicted of nudity in a public place. The man had appeared as a "go-go" dancer at the Hotel St. Paul in Abbotsford, Quebec. Clad initially in brief panties, the man removed these during his performance. He continued to dance while totally exposed. The go-go music was described as quite fast and, according to the judge, as he danced in time to it his testicles and penis swung back and forth. Some of the 60 men and women viewing this display were amused, perhaps even delighted, but others were embarrassed.

The young man was found guilty by a provincial magistrate. He appealed his conviction, which was set aside by the Quebec Court of Appeal. The Court of Appeal said that the Crown had not proven that the nude dancer had offended public decency or order. The Crown appealed the case to the Supreme Court of Canada, which restored the conviction.

The Supreme Court said that based upon the evidence in the case, the man had appeared in the nude without lawful excuse. This was enough for a conviction. The Crown was not required to show that the nudity offended public order or decency, as that went beyond the requirements of section 170. The fact that the nude dance was compatible with public standards of order or decency could not be used as a defense of lawful excuse. The only possible defense was that he was engaged in a theatrical performance. Since the young man did not raise this possibility, the Supreme Court restricted itself to the defense he had raised. The fine was $150.

As can be seen in comparing cases prosecuted as indecent acts and nudity, exhibition of all or parts of the body is not necessarily a crime. Much depends on the circumstances of each case.

## Urinating in Public and Exhibitionism

For a man to show off his private parts to an unwilling woman or a child certainly falls within the type of activities punishable under the Criminal Code. If, however, a man feels an urge to relieve himself and no toilet facility is available, is it a criminal offense for him to urinate by the roadside? Against the side of a building? In a public fountain? According to a New Brunswick court, urinating in public is not a crime.

Late one night, a man parked his car on a Fredericton street. His female companion remained in the car while he got out to relieve himself. As he was urinating behind the car, a patrol car came by. The officer stopped to ask the man what he thought he was doing. The man told him that he was "taking a leak." An altercation followed and the man was charged and convicted of indecent exposure. He appealed his conviction and won. The New Brunswick Supreme Court said that given the circumstances of the case, the man's act did not amount to a crime under the Criminal Code. Nor was it an offense under the old Common Law. Since the activity occurred out of the view of others, it did not meet the requirements for indecent exposure.

In some situations, the act of urinating in public may constitute a crime. If a young man decides to relieve himself in full view of a crowd of respectable symphony-goers outside a concert hall, that may amount to indecent exposure. The act of urinating alone is not the crime. What makes it an offense is his doing it so as to insult or offend others. Society as a whole looks disapprovingly on such a public spectacle. Well-furred and fashionably coiffed symphony-goers would likely be offended by such behavior. If, however, the young man was drunk to the point that he did not know what he was doing, he may lack the intent required for such a public display to amount to a crime of indecent exposure. Whether the act is criminal or not, therefore, depends on the facts of each case.

## Exhibitionism: The Medical Perspective

As in other areas of law and medicine, the definition and characteristics of exhibitionism are not necessarily the same. In a major study of the subject at the Clarke Institute of Psychiatry in Toronto, physicians developed a medical description of exhibitionism which is far more specific than the requirements of the Criminal Code.

According to the Clarke study, there are four elements included in the definition of exhibitionism. It is (1) the acting out of an urge or impulse, (2) by revealing the male genitals, (3) before an unsuspecting female, (4) from which the man receives sexual gratification. From this specific description of exhibitionism are excluded a number of situations, including nude sunbathing, genital exposure to another man and female exposure of the breast or vagina.

Many psychiatrists believe that the typical exhibitionist is between the ages of 20 and 30, is of average intelligence and is characteristically an underachiever. Exhibitionists come from all walks of life. Many of the exhibitionists over 21 are married, but their marital relationships are marked by tension, fights, unsatisfactory sexual relations and financial difficulties. Many frequently repeat their exhibitionist activities. It is not a onetime event.

According to psychiatrists who have studied and worked with exhibitionists, the crime will usually occur in a street, in open places such as parks or alleyways, or in cars in full view of a woman who has been drawn towards it. The exhibitionist does not attempt to touch the viewer. For the exhibitionist, the mere exposure of his genitals proves to himself and others that he is masculine, aggressive and competent.

Psychiatry has developed some techniques for helping the exhibitionist. None have been completely successful. Among the methods used are behavior therapy, learning how to interact with and date women (referred to as "courtship therapy") and drug treatment.

Not all cases follow the general pattern. It is estimated that in approximately two percent of exhibitionists, an additional feature is present. In these cases the man does not meet the strict criteria of the exhibitionist. He may use foul or abusive language, follow the victim, repeatedly expose himself to one woman, or try to touch the victim as he exposes himself. There is something which sets these men apart from the traditional exhibitionist. While this group does not necessarily have dangerous tendencies, these men may be more disturbed than others and, as a result, require special help.

## Streakers

As compared with the medical definition of the act, streaking is generally outside the scope of exhibitionism. Most streakers do not go jogging in their birthday suits to obtain sexual gratification. Most do it as a lark or in response to a dare or a bet. They do not restrict their "victims" to women as do typical exhibitionists.

Although medicine may not view streakers as exhibitionists, what about the law? Is it a crime? How have the courts handled streakers in Canada?

Streaking came into vogue in the mid-1970s throughout North America. As one judge put it, streaking became the latest in a series of rituals of spring that have included goldfish swallowing and telephone booth cramming. Unlike previous frolics, streaking gained considerable attention, including judicial review.

In 1975, a young man streaked through Taylor Field in Regina on Regina Rams Football Club Family Night. The man was caught and charged with the indecent act of running naked through the stadium. He appealed his sentence of 30 days at the Provincial Correctional Centre and won. The court said that streaking had been greeted in public with amused tolerance, even in Regina. It had not been met with alarm or outrage. For an activity to be punishable under the Criminal Code section covering indecent acts, there had to be evidence that the act involved "moral turpitude." Streaking not only lacked immorality, it also included no evidence of sexual deviation or exploitation. Without proof that streaking was immoral, the conviction had to be overturned.

Ontario also had a streaking case. One evening in March 1974, a young man was seen running through Ottawa clad in a red scarf (around his neck). He had bet some friends that he could streak downtown and purchase some beer. When a police officer stopped him and asked him what he was doing, the man replied that he was on his way to the Brewers' Retail Store. Although he pleaded guilty to an indecent act under section 169 of the Criminal Code, he changed his mind and requested permission to change his plea. He argued that he should have been charged under section 170 of the Criminal Code which prohibits nudity in a public place. Since section 170 prosecutions can only be launched with permission of the provincial attorney general, he argued that he had been denied the benefits and protection of this portion of the Criminal Code.

Judge Swabey of the Ontario Provincial Court rejected the man's argument and stated that section 169 of the Criminal Code was encompassing enough to include streaking. Streaking downtown, the judge indicated, involved a greater degree of moral turpitude than appearing nude in a public place. Since more than nudity was involved (i.e., nudity plus running), the young man had been charged correctly as violating section 169.

In deciding what should be done by way of punishment, the court noted that streaking was a new scholarly high jinks involving predominantly males in bared flight. Judge Swabey took into consideration the effect of media coverage of all that is uncovered in streaking. Given the young man's promise not to repeat his nude run, the fact that he had no previous criminal record and society's tacit approval of streaking, the court granted an absolute discharge of the conviction.

What distinctions can be drawn between streaking and exhibition-ism which would justify lenient treatment of these nude runners? One obvious distinction is that streakers intend no harm or offense to anyone. Exhibitionists prey upon unsuspecting women from whom they derive sexual gratification by watching the victim's reaction to the exposed penis. Exhibitionists intend to offend women. Another distinction is that in the mid-1970s streaking was tacitly approved or encouraged by many segments of society. Exhibitionism has never received social approval and has generally been viewed as an act of sexually deviant men.

Streaking has gone out of vogue in recent years. The novelty has worn off and the antics of those afflicted with "spring fever" have changed. Although it remains a criminal offense to zip around in the nude, the punishment awaiting streakers is little more than a slap—on the wrist.

## Who Can Expose to Whom?

The medical definition of exhibitionism excludes women from the category of would-be exhibitionists. To psychiatrists, only men can be so labeled. It also excludes men who expose themselves to other men. What about the law? Would the Criminal Code accept the medical definition and convict women of exposing themselves or men to other men?

The Criminal Code of Canada is not restricted to men only as violators of the sections dealing with indecent acts and nudity, nor does it refer to women only as victims. Instead it refers to "any person." Thus far, however, there is a scarcity of reported cases in which a woman has been charged with exhibitionism. The same holds true of male exposure to males. This lack of reported criminal cases of female exhibitionism should not be interpreted to mean that the courts will restrict it to a "male only" offense. There have been a number of scholarly articles in the United States and West Germany which suggest that female exhibitionism does exist. Some of the psychological motivations differ, but the patterns of exposure behavior are quite similar to those found among male exhibitionists. With the movement for women's equality, prosecutions for female exhibition-ism may follow.

## Peeping Toms

A different problem involves those who get a thrill or sexual gratifica-tion from peering into other people's homes. "Peeping Toms" enjoy watching others disrobing or dressing. They generally pose no threat and their behavior amounts to no more than a nuisance. The question is whether in Canada it is a crime to be a "Peeping Tom"?

In 1950, the Supreme Court of Canada held that being a "Peeping Tom" was not a criminal offense. The case which gave rise to the decision involved a British Columbia man. In March 1947, a husband was awakened by his wife, who said that his mother who lived with the couple was calling for him. His mother said she had seen a man peering in the window as she was preparing to go to bed. Acting on his mother's observation, he ran outside and gave chase to a man running from his property. He captured the man who was identified by the mother and the police were called. The "Peeping Tom" was arrested.

The Supreme Court of Canada said that neither under the Criminal Code nor at Common Law is it a crime to be a "Peeping Tom." Even though looking in on a woman preparing for bed may provoke the inhabitants to violence or retaliation, this does not make peeping a crime. Adding insult to injury, the Supreme Court said that the man who had been collared by the property owner was entitled to damages for false imprisonment since, there being no crime in peeping, he had been improperly detained.

"Peeping Toms," exhibitionists and others involved in indecent exposure may all have some psychological problem. Although offensive to others, they usually are no threat to society. The law and medicine have recognized this by drawing distinctions in diagnosis, treatment and punishment between exhibitionists, rapists and child molesters. This is a little comfort to those who have seen what they ought not, and to those who have been seen when they ought not have been.

# 14 Sex on Stage, Screen, Television, Radio and in Print

To many people obscenity means sexual hang-ups, perversion, men in trench coats, porno shops, adult movies, whips, chains, throwing glasses across a bar and of course, Toronto's Yonge Street.

Why is it that society associates obscenity with perversion, rapists and molesters of choir boys? Why does government try to clamp down on films, magazines, books and devices which it deems filthy or obscene, but that vast numbers of people want to see? What authority do the provincial governments possess in controlling the dissemination of this material? How does it differ from the requirements of the Criminal Code and other federal laws? What other types of government pressure are used to control "smut?" Can a private person enjoy "blue" movies or "dirty" books in his own home without fear of government intrusion? What happened to freedom of speech? The answers to many of these questions may raise more eyebrows than the material which government and we as a society seek to regulate.

## The Reasons for Government Regulation

It is difficult to pinpoint the exact reasons that support government control of obscene material. By far, the most frequently voiced rationale is that it prevents the disintegration of society. As Lord Devlin suggested in 1965, historically, the relaxation of moral standards has signaled the decline of society. Therefore, society is justified in instituting measures which preserve and protect its moral fiber. This would include the suppression of vices such as obscenity. Whether obscenity really does destroy society is an open question. Some say it strengthens it by providing a harmless emotional outlet.

Further arguments for the control of obscene materials are to protect the impressionable young and to dampen the latent perversive behavior of sexual psychopaths. As the Law Reform Commission of Canada pointed out in one of its working papers, it was possible for some Ottawa children to deposit 25 cents in a peep-show machine and view all sorts of sexual activity. The machines were installed in a variety store near a number of schools. The incest scene of one flick left the impression that the children could get their fathers to engage in sexual activity with them and that such behavior was not only quite normal—but fun. No studies were done as to whether the children asked their fathers.

The evidence is not conclusive that viewing arousing sex films triggers sexual psychopaths to perform criminal acts such as rape. There could be a variety of factors which set off such individuals.

The argument regarding children is another matter. Government has a special duty to make certain—almost like a super-parent—that children are protected. Given the way in which children can be easily swayed, it is important to allow parents and government alike to control unwanted and perhaps damaging impressions. It is for this reason more than any other that government can justify the regulation of obscene materials.

## What is Regulated?

Almost every type of obscene material is regulated. Movies, books magazines, devices, television and radio programming are all subject to control. So are live "performances" such as topless go-go dancers and male strippers. The controls extend to movie theatres, drive-ins and live theatres and night clubs. Even the mailing of obscene materials is subject to regulation.

The sources of legal control are many and varied. Some regulation is found within the Criminal Code of Canada. Other laws are in the statutes and regulations of the Canadian Radio and Television Commission, the provincial censorship boards and Customs Canada. With this array of authorities charged with regulating obscene material, it is rather difficult at times to pinpoint exactly the extent of each legal authority.

On numerous occasions, the authoratative scope of government has been called into question. In a variety of court cases, people have challenged what they see as unwarranted, "big-brother-like" intrusions into their lives and livelihoods. In a few cases, the courts have agreed and stated that the government went too far.

In one Alberta case, *R.* v. *Harrision,* some people were charged with violating the obscenity prohibition in the Criminal Code. They had shown an allegedly obscene movie to 25 men in a community hall. Outside the room was a notice that within was a private party. The court held that it was improper to have charged the men with criminal offenses. For a crime to occur, the court said, the law requires publication, that is, the showing of obscene material to others. Revealing supposedly obscene material to those specifically invited to see it does not constitute publication.

In an Ontario case. *R.* v. *Schell,* the court ruled on an obscenity charge against a man who had been accused of making obscene photographs. In court, it was determined that he had taken the photos for his own private use. Without intending publication of the photos, the man was well within his rights and the charges were dismissed. As long as the obscene material is for one's own use or that of one's friends, it will usually escape the clutches of the law. Even the slightest publication, however, could trigger criminal charges.

## Obscenity

Laws regulating obscene publications and performances have been a part of the Criminal Code since the 1890s. Prior to that time, in 1868, the Common Law laid down a working definition of obscenity. In *R.* v. *Hicklin,* the court said that obscenity is material which has the tendency to "deprave and corrupt those whose minds are open to such immoral influences and into whose hands a publication of this sort may fall." This became known as the *Hicklin* test.

Over the years, Canadian courts have applied this test to allegedly obscene films, live performances, books and magazines. Many of these decisions generated a considerable amount of criticism, although the focus of the criticism was not so much on the decisions as it was on the *Hicklin* test. Opponents to the rule claimed that it was highly subjective and loaded with vague and often inconsistent criteria. Others argued that the rule made it too easy for the Crown prosecutor to prove that something was obscene. Rather than basing a decision on the average citizen, the rule was aimed at the most unsophisticated audience. Furthermore, the courts tended to zoom in on isolated passages of books or film clippings without considering the overall value or purpose of the work.

With this ground swell of criticism, Parliament decided to correct the situation. In 1959, the Criminal Code was modified to include a definition of obscenity. Section 159 (B) defines "obscenity" for the purposes of the Criminal Code as "any publication a dominant characteristic of which is the undue exploitation of sex, or of sex any one or more of the following subjects, namely crime, horror, cruelty and violence." The Minister of Justice at the time, Mr. Fulton, claimed that the new statutory definition would provide the courts with an objective test of obscenity. In this way, he continued, decisions would be more swift and certain. It was believed that the courts would be more disposed to hand down convictions than was the case previously.

Despite the action taken by Parliament, uncertainty persisted. In his speeches, Mr. Fulton pointed out that the old *Hicklin* test for obscenity would still apply in certain cases. It would be used to determine the existence of obscene material where it was contended that publications had a genuine literary, artistic or scientific merit.

Until 1978, it was uncertain whether the new statutory definition of obscenity supplemented or superseded the *Hicklin* requirements. Thanks to an Ontario case, it is now generally believed that the old *Hicklin* test is no longer applicable. In that case, police raided a sex shop, "Erotique Ltd.," in St. Catharines. The proprietor, Mr. Duchow, was charged with violating that section of the Criminal Code which prohibited the possession of obscene material with the intent to distribute it. Police took note of a variety of sex aids and stimulators that were available for purchase. With each item in the display window, they noted, were signs explaining the purpose of each device. Mr. Duchow was convicted and appealed the case. His case went all the way to the Supreme Court of Canada.

The Supreme Court upheld Mr. Duchow's conviction. In doing so, however, the justices cleared away some of the confusion surrounding the definition of obscenity. The court found that the definition in the Criminal Code, which refers to "publication," was applicable to the sex aids found in Mr. Duchow's shop. The aftermath of the decision was to completely discard the old *Hicklin* obscenity test, at least in criminal cases.

Critics of the Criminal Code definition of obscenity have argued that while the consideration of each case now focuses on the entire work or object, its content, purpose and merit is no less subjective than the old definition. It is unlikely that the courts or Parliament will ever come up with a definition that will satisfy all people. Value judgements and social norms are not consistent. The best the courts can do is assess what is the consensus of the community's norms and values. Although this too is not objective. Courts depend on the evidence presented in each case and each party puts forth testimony of experts and documents which best support their arguments. Judges also bring to each case their own morality and values. As objective as they try to be, their backgrounds may color their thinking. No definition or decision-making process will be totally satisfactory as long as it is based on a consensus of communal beliefs.

## The Criminal Code

Putting aside the problem of defining obscenity, it is important to understand what types of materials and activities may fall prey to the Criminal Code. Four different sections of the Code are of importance. These laws cover offenses which tend to corrupt morals, the seizure of obscene material, immoral theatrical performances and the mailing of obscene materials.

## Obscenity for Sale: Section 159 of the Criminal Code

Section 159 is very extensive in what it includes as prohibited activities. Such things as the printing, publishing, distributing or circulating of obscene written material, pictures, films, records and the like are subject to criminal sanctions. It is an offense under the Criminal Code to see or offer to sell, to expose or have in one's possession with the intent to expose, obscene materials. Obscenity is assessed by the statutory definition described earlier.

Section 159 also punishes those who make, possess, print, sell, distribute or intend to do these acts with a "crime comic." A crime comic is a magazine, book or periodical largely composed of material describing in pictures, crimes or events connected with the commission of crimes. Section 159 applies whether the crimes represented in the photos are fictitious or real.

A series of defenses are set out in section 159 which may be used by defendants. If an individual can prove that the "public good" was served by his actions and that his conduct does not exceed that which is required to serve the public good, he cannot be convicted of corrupting morals.

Certain defenses are not available. A defendant cannot allege ignorance of the nature or presence of the obscene material. The lack of these defenses, however, does not make it any more difficult for a person charged with corrupting morals to defend himself than a person charged with robbery.

The prosecutor needs a considerable amount of evidence to gain a conviction under this portion of the Criminal Code. This was apparent shortly after the Criminal Code was changed to include a definition of obscenity. The Supreme Court of Canada held in 1962 that the novel *Lady Chatterly's Lover* did not contain undue exploitation of sex. The Court said that authors need latitude in the writing of books with genuine literary merit. Taking this into account, the Court stated, the statutory definition of obscenity must have some relevance if it is to be applied in such cases. It was inapplicable to this novel.

Proving undue exploitation of sex is difficult. The courts have interpreted this requirement of the statutory definition of obscenity to be measured by contemporary community standards in Canada. It also requires consideration of the artistic merit of the work and, in the case of a film, the producer's purpose.

In measuring the community's expectation, courts have viewed it as a test of tolerance, of just how much freedom of exposure society will grant. The manner and circumstances in which material is distributed influence this assessment. Indiscriminate exposure of offensive material to those who do not wish to see it would violate the standard of tolerance. Distribution or exposure to a certain segment of the community who want such material would be permissible. The Ontario case of *R.* v. *The MacMillan Company of Canada, Ltd.* illustrates this approach to community standards.

The publishing company was charged with producing an obscene text called *Show Me.* It was a book of detailed photographs of naked people's genitalia. The court dismissed the case on the basis that the price and distribution plan for the book precluded indiscriminate exposure of it. The court said that the community would tolerate the selective use of the text by parents in providing their children with sex education information.

## Obscenity Seized: Section 160 of the Criminal Code

Section 160 of the Criminal Code allows for the seizure and forfeiture of materials deemed obscene. There are certain procedures that law enforcement officers must meet in order to confiscate material believed to be obscene. It includes a requirement to obtain from a judge a warrant or court order allowing officers to take the material. The owner and author of the material have a right to a court hearing to determine whether the material is obscene. If the court determines that it is, the publication is forfeited to Her Majesty. If the court finds that it is not obscene, the articles must be returned to the owner.

## Theatre of the Obscene: Section 163 of the Criminal Code

Section 163 of the Criminal Code applies to immoral theatrical performances. Under this provision, the manager, agent or the person in charge of a theatre would be guilty of violating the law if he allows or presents an immoral, indecent or obscene performance. Similarly, actors, performers and those who assist them would be guilty of a crime if they participated in such a performance.

Under the terms of the immoral theatrical performances section of the Criminal Code, it would seem that stage plays such as *Hair* and *Equus* could have been closed before they opened. Their producers, directors and actors would be languishing in Canadian prisons from coast to coast. Plays like *Who's Afraid of Virginia Wolf* would be barred and Toronto theatres would instead stage *Mary Poppins*. Courts have not taken such drastic steps. Much latitude in fact has been given theatrical entertainment. One case that illustrates the point is *Johnson* v. *The Queen.*

Miss Johnson was arrested for participating in a nude performance in violation of section 163 of the Criminal Code. She had performed a strip tease to the point that she was completely nude. A police officer who witnessed the act in Dino's Hideaway in Calgary testified that the defendant did nothing offensive other than being naked. Following her conviction and a series of appeals, the Supreme Court of Canada overturned the guilty verdict.

The Supreme Court said that an act or performance does not become "immoral" simply because it has been made an offense by Parliament. A nude performance, therefore, is not automatically immoral and a criminal offense. It requires more than the display of nudity for a theatrical performance to be deemed immoral or indecent under section 163.

## Mail Obscenity: Section 164 of the Criminal Code

Another important section of the Criminal Code deals with mailing obscene material. Section 164 makes it a crime to use the mail to transmit or deliver anything that is obscene, immoral or scurrilous. Even private letters intended only for the recipient fall within the scope of this law. A highly publicized Ontario case involving this section of the Criminal Code focused on a gay newspaper.

In *R.* v. *Pink Triangle Press,* the paper was charged with transmitting indecent, immoral and scurrilous material through the mail. The newspaper, *Body Politic,* carried a detailed news item about homosexual activities between men and young boys. The Crown prosecutor brought charges claiming that the story fell within the sanctions of section 164.

Provincial Court Judge Sydney Harris said that a conviction could not be based on immorality, since the Criminal Code does not define that term. He said it was so ambiguous and vague that no person could be expected to conduct himself by such an imprecise standard. The judge said that what is important is the treatment of the subject. The topic is not important. If the treatment of the subject is not indecent, there can be no conviction. This would hold true even if the topic was shocking to the community.

Judge Harris's decision was later overruled by the county court and by the Ontario Court of Appeal. It was clearly determined that the judge must apply the standards of the community to the material in question. The judge makes up his own mind as to what those standards are, as difficult as such a decision may be.

## Proving Criminal Obscenity

Even if the Criminal Code included precise definitions for community standards in section 164, or for that matter in sections 159, 160 and 163, there would still be the problem of how to apply these interpretations. Taking the pulse of community standards is not an easy task as they shift from day to day. And what is the community?

Since it pops up as a criminal matter, prosecutors must produce evidence which proves, beyond a reasonable doubt, that the defendant violated the law. This too is no easy task, especially when the subject matter of the law is ill-defined. Perhaps the cumbersome, unworkable nature of the criminal law explains why the Canadian Radio and Television Commission and the provinces have opted for censorship or rating programs.

## The Importation of Obscene Material

The importing of obscene material into Canada is regulated by the Customs Act and by the Customs Tariff Act. Under the Customs Act, a Customs officer may detain those goods which are prohibited, controlled or regulated by or under any Act of Parliament. Thus materials which would violate the Criminal Code, the Post Office Act or the Customs Tariff Act could be held and disposed of in the manner set forth in this legislation.

Under the Customs Tariff Act, there is a list of so-called "prohibited goods" which includes books, printed material, drawings, paintings, prints, photographs and other representations considered to be of an immoral or indecent character. Under the Customs Act, if a book or other imported item is considered prohibited on this basis, there is a right to have the decision reviewed by a court. According to the Customs Tariff Act, prohibited goods are forfeited to the Crown and the importer is liable for a fine of up to $300.

There have been some interesting cases involving these laws. In *R. v. Paterson,* the defendants attempted to use the Customs entry permit for some publications as a defense to a criminal charge of unlawfully distributing obscene material in Ottawa. The Ontario Court of Appeal rejected the argument, saying that the fact that Customs had screened and allowed the material in could not serve as a defense to charges under the Criminal Code. The conclusion can only be that what is obscene under the Criminal Code may not be obscene under the Customs Act.

In another case *Re Winkler and Deputy Minister of National Revenue,* a man challenged a Customs ban on the importation of two books and lost. The books, *Oral Sex* and *Law and Decision in Denmark,* were found to be immoral and obscene, as each contained over 170 sexual illustrations. The larger portion of the illustrations were full-page photographs portraying what the court described as "sex in its most lurid form." Accordingly, the court upheld the ban on the importation of the books. In that case the defendant did not get a chance to commit the crime of sending obscene material through the mails. He was not even allowed to bring it into Canada.

There is one other important law regarding the importation of goods. Found under the Post Office Act, it authorizes postal employees to turn over to a Customs officer for examination all mail from outside Canada containing or suspected of containing anything which is prohibited or subject to customs. In this situation, the Customs officer is permitted to open all mail other than letters. Suspected letters may be opened either by the addressee with the Customs officer present or, with the addressee's written permission, the Customs officer may open the letter himself. If the Customs officer finds that any mail contains nonmailable material, including obscene magazines, it is turned over to the Post Office to deal with under postal regulations. Should the addressee either refuse to open a suspected letter or decline to allow the Customs officer to do so, it is then treated as undeliverable mail.

The authority given Customs and Post Canada in controlling indecent and immoral material is not the same as that given police under the Criminal Code. It is a noncriminal type of regulation designed to *prevent entry* into Canada of such matter. The Criminal Code tries to *prevent distribution* of obscene material by threatening to punish the person spreading it about.

## Classification and Censorship of Obscene Matter

The Criminal Code and the Federal Customs and Post Office rules are not the only mechanisms available for controlling obscene material. The Canadian Radio and Television Commission has adopted laws restricting broadcasts of obscene programs. Some of the provinces have also adopted film classification laws or created censorship boards which control pornographic movies. Not unlike the Criminal Code, the definitions and standards for determining obscenity are vague and imprecise.

## The CRTC and Obscenity

Television and radio are among the most highly regulated industries in Canada. Complete freedom of speech on the air is a myth. The regulations issued by the CRTC are very specific and include exact requirements for what can and cannot be heard on radio and seen on television. Even the types of programs and the content of each are considered in the regulations.

There are three different sets of regulations for television, AM radio and FM radio. All three prohibit the broadcasting of anything contrary to law as well as any obscene, indecent or profane language. Promotional programs believed to be of an offensive or an objectionable nature may also be banned from the airways. A representative of the CRTC must give the station notice and ask the station to show why the promotional program should remain unchanged. If the station cannot give an adequate reason, the CRTC can order that the program be modified.

According to the Broadcasting Act which created it, the CRTC has the power to revoke and suspend a broadcasting license. It may do so after a hearing when it is satisfied that the licensee has violated or failed to comply with the regulations and the terms of its license. A disgruntled licensee has a right to appeal to a court.

The problem, as in all legislation which tries to control obscenity, is that neither the Broadcasting Act nor the regulations contain any definitions of "obscene, indecent or profane language." The CRTC must make their own determination of what language would meet these criteria. Words which ten or 15 years ago would have been considered obscene or indecent are now commonly used in everyday speech. Society has become more tolerant of such language, particularly for adults. But what about children? Should they be exposed to obscene or indecent language? Why should the CRTC be concerned if children are already familiar with this language from their friends? How far can the CRTC go in being society's protector? The CRTC, in picking out obscene, indecent or profane language, has quite a task before it. Given the shifting sands of society's tolerance and acceptance of foul words, it is a thankless and largely impossible job.

The CRTC may have an easier time of it in enforcing the ban against programs which are contrary to law. The broadcast of written material or a play that has already been found by the courts to be obscene under the Criminal Code would likely be banned by the CRTC. It would come within the regulation which prohibits broadcasts "contrary to the law." Suppose, however, the CRTC disagrees with the law courts and does not believe a book is obscene or a play immoral. Could a radio station broadcast a reading of the book? Could a television station televise the play? Despite its objection to the court's decision, the CRTC would likely be hamstrung and forced to ban the broadcasts. The courts, by finding the book or play obscene under the Criminal Code, would almost force the CRTC to classify a broadcast of either one as contrary to law. In the end, the CRTC is placed in the unenviable position of the heavy-handed censor.

## Provincial Classification and Rating Boards

People often confuse obscenity legislation with censorship. Frequently, the control of obscenity is treated as synonymous with censorship. In actuality, each term represents a different approach to the same problem: how to control objectionable or pornographic material. Basically, censorship controls the existence of the objectionable material, whereas obscenity laws regulate the circumstances in which it may be displayed. The courts have stated that obscenity laws are federal and censorship laws are provincial.

Each province has its own way of regulating "adult" films. In a number of provinces, a film must be submitted to the board of censors for review prior to exhibiting or advertising it. In Manitoba, New Brunswick and Saskatchewan, the censorship board assigns a classification to the films. In Manitoba the classifications include "general," "mature," "adult parental guidance" and "restricted adult." New Brunswick uses the classification "restricted." Saskatchewan uses the designations "general," "adult," and "restricted adult."

The category in which a film is placed affects the type of audience who can see it and the advertising used to promote it. In New Brunswick, Ontario and British Columbia, a film with a "restricted" rating means that people less than 18 years of age cannot view it. Saskatchewan has a similar 18 years of age policy for films rated "special X." Films with restricted classifications usually require some symbol or notice as part of newspaper or broadcast advertising. Some of the censorship boards have the added authority to control what film clips of a "coming feature" may be shown in a theater or what photos may be used in a poster.

New Brunswick, British Columbia and some other provinces also grant the censors the authority to delete segments of the film. Once a film is approved by a censorship board, it cannot be altered nor can another version of the film be substituted for it. The only exception is the repairing of defective footage.

In British Columbia and Manitoba, theater owners and film associations disturbed with the ruling of a provincial censorship board are specifically given the right to challenge the rating. There is a procedure for appeal in these and other provinces set out in the film classification board laws and regulations. Even in provinces without specific appeal procedures, disgruntled theater owners and film distributors still have the right to a court challenge.

The failure to obtain approval or a rating for a film prior to exhibiting it could result in serious difficulty. Many of the provinces consider it an offense and still have fines and jail sentences for offenders.

As the censorship system operates throughout the provinces, it is geared towards restricting certain audiences—mainly young people —from viewing what is considered objectionable or overly provocative material for them. It also provides movie patrons with an idea of what they can expect before they enter the theater. Like the Criminal Code ban on obscenity, the censorship system is not perfect. To people conscious of freedom of expression, censorship smacks of unwanted government control. To its proponents, the system is a workable solution to the problem of restricting unsavory films from young people and sensitive adults.

## Other "Controls" of Objectionable Materials

To many film distributors, theater owners and film syndicates, the costs and time spent on clearing a film with a provincial censorship board is just not worth it. For them, it is easier not to appeal an unfavorable rating or rejection and to submit a watered-down version to the censors. The legal fees and adverse publicity generated by challenging a censorship board's decision are key considerations, though in some cases, the publicity can be profitable if the film is eventually shown. It means that the provincial censorship and film rating laws have a far greater impact than what is set out in the statutes and regulations.

The same is true of the Criminal Code laws on obscenity. Police and Crown prosecutors can threaten prosecution under the Criminal Code to keep theatrical promoters and book distributors in check, even if the prosecution would not be successful. For many people, the embarrassment and damage to their personal reputation resulting from a criminal charge is enough to deter them from violating the obscenity laws. Others may be more brazen, knowing that the uncertainity of standards and definition of obscenity in the Criminal Code fall heavily in favor of the defendant. They are often in the minority.

Another form of control is to localize in one area the objectionable movie houses, book shops, strip joints and massage parlors. Boston did this in their so-called "combat zone." The idea was to keep those who offer such services and their customers away from the rest of the community who find them objectionable. The police thought it would aid them in enforcing the law. Other North American cities have considered or attempted to establish such zones. This "live and let live" policy does not always work and could backfire into more serious policing problems. It may not be possible to accommodate the interests of both the community at large and the patrons of the "zone."

## The Pursuit of Filth

The arguments against laws restricting freedom of expression and freedom of reading, viewing and attending are all related to the individual. The words of Lord Devlin regarding the moral fiber of society seem stuffy and out of date. However, the obscenity debate raises a major social, political and legal question in our society. Are the wishes of society to overrule those of the individual? If the matter of obscenity was simply one of taste, the issue would not be so important. The fact that the majority does not like a particular film because it extols what most feel is immorality, is no reason to prevent those who want to see it from doing so. There is no evidence to show that the occasional "dirty" book (by this year's standards), or pornographic film, ever hurt the patrons or society as a whole.

What is really feared is that complete freedom will encourage and develop a taste for this particular type of expression, thus changing, and in fact endangering, the current social taste. The fear is that all movie houses will show pornographic films and by doing so starve out those catering to the current taste of the majority. A proliferation of films, books and television programs may inundate the current cultural standards of the majority of people in society. Does the majority have the right to protect itself from this potential change by restricting the freedom of the minority?

In fact, this is often done without law, as is shown by the difficulties experienced by the producers of the plays *Luther* and *The Deputy* in renting theaters in Catholic-dominated Montreal some years ago. The question is: Should such a right be enforced by law? And if so, how effective will it be?

The law of obscenity is not a precise set of statutes and regulations. The number of Canadian courts that have struggled with what is and is not obscene is proof of this uncertainty. It will likely remain a problem as long as society is inconsistent about its social and moral judgments. In the meantime, courts and censorship boards will have to carry on their tasks.

# 15 For Help in Good Times and Bad....

Many people may have questions, concerns or problems involving sex. Some of these questions may have legal implications. To assist readers in finding organizations or groups to aid them, the following lists of organizations are provided. It should be noted that hundreds of other groups exist, many in smaller communities throughout Canada. It would not be practical in this book to list them all. Instead a selected list of major metropolitan and regional offices has been provided.

A Word About Accuracy of the Lists. These lists were prepared in December 1980, prior to the book going to print. It is possible that some of the organizations listed no longer exist or have moved.

## BIRTHRIGHT

This organization is a birth counseling group. As part of its stated philosophy, it is against abortion. In addition to those listed, it has many offices or contacts in smaller Canadian communities.

**Founding Headquarters and Ontario Regional Consultant**
Mrs. Louise Summerhill, Founder and Director
Birthright
761 Coxwell Avenue
Toronto, Ontario M4C 3C5
(416) 469-1111

**Alberta Regional Consultant**
Birthright
108, 11520-100 Avenue
Edmonton, Alberta T6A 2C8

**British Columbia Regional Consultant**
Birthright
207 West Hastings, Apt. 902
Vancouver, British Columbia V6B 1H7
(604) 669-0731

**Saskatchewan Regional Consultant**
Birthright
105-1855 Scarth Street
Regina, Saskatchewan S4P 2G9
(306) 525-6669

**Quebec Regional Consultant**
Birthright
1800 Dorchester Street West
Montreal, Quebec H3H 2H2
(514) 937-9324

**Atlantic Provinces Regional Consultant**
Birthright
10-5211 Blowers Street, # 310
Halifax, Nova Scotia B3J 1J5
(902) 422-4408

## GAY RIGHTS AND TRANSSEXUAL ORGANIZATIONS

In this list are included a variety of selected gay and transsexual groups. Some of the addresses given include both mailing and street addresses. The organizations listed offer social, political, legal, informational and medical assistance.

**British Columbia**
Gay Alliance Towards Equality (GATE)
Box 1463, Station A
Vancouver, British Columbia V6C 2P7
(604) 683-3832

Society for Education, Action, Research and Counselling
in Homosexuality (SEARCH)
Box 48903
Bentall Centre
Vancouver, British Columbia V7X 1A8
(604) 689-1039

## Alberta

Gay Information and Resources Calgary (GIRC)
Old Y Building, Suites 317-323
223-12 Avenue, S.W.
Calgary, Alberta T2P 0G9
(403) 264-3911

Gay Alliance Towards Equality (GATE)
Box 1852
Edmonton, Alberta T5J 2P2
(403) 424-8361

## Saskatchewan

Regina Gay Community Centre
2242 Smith Street
Regina, Saskatchewan S4P 2P4
(306) 522-7343

Gay Community Centre
Box 1662
245-Third Avenue
Saskatoon, Saskatchewan S7K 3R8
(306) 652-0972

Lesbian Caucus, Saskatoon Women's Liberation
Box 4021
Saskatoon, Saskatchewan S7K 3T1

Subcommittee on Gay Rights
Saskatchewan Association on Human Rights
311-20 Street, West
Saskatoon, Saskatchewan S7M 0X1
(306) 244-1933

## Manitoba

Gays for Equality
Box 27, UMSU
University of Manitoba
Winnipeg, Manitoba R3T 2N2
(204) 269-8678

Manitoba Physicians for Homosexual Understanding
Box 3911, Station B
Winnipeg, Manitoba R2W 5H9

## Ontario

Foundation for the Advancement of Canadian Transsexuals (FACT)
Box 1497, Station C
Kitchener, Ontario N2G 4P2

Gay Rights Organization of Waterloo
Box 2632, Station B
Kitchener, Ontario N2H 6N2

Foundation for the Advancement of Canadian Transsexuals (FACT)
Box 4724, Station D
London, Ontario N5W 5L7
(519) 644-1061

Homophile Association of London, Ontario (HALO)
649 Colborne Street
London, Ontario N6A 3Z2
(519) 433-3762

London Lesbian Collective
Box 4724, Station D
London, Ontario N5W 5L7

Gays of Ottawa/Gais de l'Outaouais
Box 2191, Station D
GO Centre, 175 Lisgar Street
Ottawa, Ontario K1P 5W9
(613) 233-0152

Foundation for the Advancement of Canadian Transsexuals (FACT)
618-2757 Kipling Avenue
Rexdale, Ontario M9V 4C4
(416) 745-5462

Gay Community Services Centre
29 Granby Street
Toronto, Ontario M5B 1H8
(416) 977-9835

Gay Liberation Union (GLU)
Box 793, Station A
Toronto, Ontario M4T 2N7
(416) 363-4410

Hassle Free Clinic
556 Church Street (at Wellesley)
Second Floor
Toronto, Ontario M4Y 2E3
(416) 922-0566 (women)
(416) 922-0603 (men)

Lesbian Organization of Toronto (LOOT)
Box 70, Station F
Toronto, Ontario M4Y 2L4
(416) 960-3249

### Québec

Association Gaie de l'Ouest Québécois (AGOQ)
CP 1215, Succ B
Hull, Québec J8X 3X7
(819) 778-1737

Association pour les droits de la communauté gaie du Québec (ADGA)
CP 36, Succ C
1264 rue St. Timothée
Montréal, Québec H2H 4J7
(514) 843-8671

Coop-Femmes
CP 223, Succ Delorimier
Montréal, Québec H2H 2N6
(514) 843-8998

Gay Health Clinic
Montreal Youth Clinic/Clinic des Jeunes de Montréal
3658 rue Ste-Famille
Montréal, Québec H2X 2L5
(514) 843-7885

Women's Information and Referral Centre
3585 rue Ste Urbain
Montréal, Québec H2X 2N6
(514) 842-4781

Centre Homophile d'Aide et de Libération (CHAL)
CP 596, Succ Haute-Ville
175 rue Prince Edouard
Quebec, Québec G1R 4R8
(418) 525-4997

## New Brunswick

Fredericton Lesbians and Gays (FLAG)
Box 1556, Station A
Fredericton, New Brunswick E3B 5G2
(506) 454-8130

## Nova Scotia

Gay Alliance for Equality Inc. (GAE)
Box 3611
Halifax South Postal Station
Halifax, Nova Scotia B3J 3K6
(902) 429-4294

## Newfoundland

Community Homophile Association of Newfoundland (CHAN)
Box 613, Station C
St. John's, Newfoundland A1C 5K8

# HUMAN RIGHTS COMMISSIONS

This list includes the address and telephone numbers of all provincial government human rights offices. They should be contacted directly with questions and complaints involving human rights law.

### British Columbia

British Columbia Human Rights Commission
Human Rights Code
Department of Labour
Parliament Buildings
Victoria, British Columbia V8V 1X4
(604) 387-6861

### Alberta

Alberta Human Rights Commission
501 Edwards Professional Building
10053-111 Street
Edmonton, Alberta T5K 0G2
(403) 427-7661

### Saskatchewan

Saskatchewan Human Rights Commission
219A-21 Street E.
Saskatoon, Saskatchewan S7K 0B7
(306) 664-3127

### Manitoba

Manitoba Human Rights Commission
200-323 Portage Avenue
Winnipeg, Manitoba R3B 2C1
(204) 944-3007

### Ontario

Ontario Human Rights Commission
400 University Avenue
Toronto, Ontario M7A 1T7
(416) 965-6841

## Québec

Quebec Human Rights Commission
611-360 St. Jacques
Montréal, Québec H2Y 1P5
(514) 873-5146

## New Brunswick

New Brunswick Human Rights Commission
P.O. Box 6000
Fredericton, New Brunswick E3B 5H1
(506) 453-2301

## Nova Scotia

Nova Scotia Human Rights Commission
P.O. Box 2221
Halifax, Nova Scotia B3J 3C4
(902) 424-4111

## Prince Edward Island

Human Rights Commission
P.O. Box 2000
Charlottetown, Prince Edward Island C1A 7N8
(902) 894-7797

## Newfoundland

Human Rights Commission
Dept. of Manpower and Industrial Relations
Government of Newfoundland and Labrador
P.O. Box 4247
St. John's, Newfoundland A1C 5Z7
(709) 754-0690    722-0711

# PLANNED PARENTHOOD

This organization is involved in the publication of and giving of advice on family planning and contraception. It is an international organization with headquarters in London, England and with many offices throughout Canada.

## British Columbia

Executive Director
Planned Parenthood Association of British Columbia
101-96 East Broadway
Vancouver, British Columbia V5T 1V6
(604) 872-8737

## Alberta

Executive Director
Planned Parenthood Alberta
#206, 233-12 Avenue, S.W.
Calgary, Alberta T2R 0G9
(403) 265-3360

## Saskatchewan

Executive Director
Planned Parenthood Saskatchewan
404-245 Third Avenue South
Saskatoon, Saskatchewan S7K 1M4
(306) 664-2050

## Manitoba

Executive Director
Planned Parenthood Manitoba
1000-259 Portage
Winnipeg, Manitoba R3B 2A9
(204) 943-6489

## Ontario

Executive Director
Planned Parenthood Ontario
P.O. Box 831
Waterloo, Ontario N2J 4C2

## Quebec

Director
La Fédération du Québec pour le planning des naissances
3826 rue St. Hubert
Montreal, Quebec H2L 4A5
(514) 842-9501

## New Brunswick

Executive Director
Planned Parenthood New Brunswick Inc.
43 Brunswick Street, Victoria Health Centre
Fredericton, New Brunswick E3B 1G5
(506) 454-1808

## Nova Scotia

Executive Director
Planned Parenthood Association of Nova Scotia
1815 Hollis Street
Halifax, Nova Scotia B3J 1W3
(902) 423-2090

## Prince Edward Island

Executive Director
Planned Parenthood of P.E.I.
218 Kent Street
Charlottetown, Prince Edward Island C1A 4B6
(902) 892-8141

## Newfoundland

Executive Director
Planned Parenthood of Newfoundland/Labrador
Fort William Building
21 Factory Lane
St. John's, Newfoundland A1C 3J8
(709) 753-7333

**Northwest Territories**

Director
Planned Parenthood Northwest Territories
P.O. Box 1680
Yellowknife, Northwest Territories X1A 2P3
(403) 873-6112

**Yukon**

Yukon Planned Parenthood
207 Elliot Street
Whitehorse, Yukon Y1A 2A1
(403) 667-2970

# WOMEN'S RIGHTS ORGANIZATIONS

In this list are included selected organizations whose goal is to better the position and rights of women in Canada. Also included are groups whose function is to assist victims of rape and clarify the other sexual assaults.

**National Action Committee on the Status of Women**
306-40 Saint Clair Avenue East
Toronto, Ontario M4T 1M9
(416) 922-3246

**Canadian Association of Sexual Assault Centres**
4-45 Kingsway
Vancouver, British Columbia V5T 3H7

# COUNCILS ON THE STATUS OF WOMEN

**Alberta**
Alberta Women's Bureau
1402 Centennial Building
10015-103 Avenue
Edmonton, Alberta T5J 0H1

### Saskatchewan

Advisory Council on the Status of Women
c/o Women's Division
Dept. of Labour
3130—8th Street East
Saskatoon, Saskatchewan S7H 0W2

### Ontario

Status of Women Council
700 Bay Street
Third Floor
Toronto, Ontario M5G 1Z6

### Quebec

Conseil du Statut de la femme
700 boul. St-Cyrille est
16-ième étage
Québec, Québec G1R 5A9

### New Brunswick

Advisory Council on the Status of Women
384 St. George Street
Moncton, New Brunswick E1C 1X2

### Nova Scotia

Advisory Council on the Status of Women
P.O. Box 745
Halifax, Nova Scotia B3J 2T3

### Prince Edward Island

Advisory Council on the Status of Women
Box 2000
Charlottetown, Prince Edward Island C1A 7N8

# Additional Readings

The following is a selected list of Canadian books which, in whole or in part, discuss Canadian law related to sex. Readers who wish to do further research on the subject should also refer to books and articles published in Canada and abroad on the psychological, sociological, cultural and moral aspects of sex.

Advisory Council on the Status of Women, *"Rape and Sexual Assault"* (Ottawa: Donelan Productions, 1976)

A. Bernadot and R. P. Kouri, *La Responsibilité Civile Medicale"* (Sherbrooke, Qué.: Les Editions Revue de Droit Université de Sherbrooke, 1980)

L. Delude, *"Abortion in Canada: background notes on the proposed amendments to the Criminal Code"* (Ottawa: Advisory Council on the Status of Women, 1975)

B. M. Dickens, *"Medico-Legal Aspects of Family Law"* (Toronto: Butterworths, 1979)

Law Reform Commission of Canada, *"Limits of Criminal Law; obscenity: a test case"* (Ottawa: Information Canada, 1975)

Law Reform Commission of Canada, *"Obscenity"* (Ottawa, Law Reform Commission of Canada, 1972)

Law Reform Commission of Canada, *"Sterilization: working paper 24"* (Ottawa: Law Reform Commission of Canada, 1979)

E. I. Picard, *"Legal Liability of Doctors and Hospitals in Canada"* (Toronto: Carswell, 1978)

Report of the Committee on the Operation of the Abortion Law (Ottawa: Supply and Services Canada, 1977)

L. E. Rozovsky, *"Canadian Hospital Law, 2nd Edition"* (Ottawa: Canadian Hospital Association, 1979)

L. E. Rozovsky, *"The Canadian Patient's Book of Rights"* (Toronto: Doubleday Canada, 1980)

G. Tarrab, Ed., *"La polémique québécoise autour de la question de l'avortement et l'affaire Morgentaler"* (Montréal: Editions Aquila, 1975)

# Index